Praise for Sarah Ruhl and Ma.

"Tender . . . A strange and beautiful volume . . . *Letters from Max* suggests ᴜ.
Ritvo's imagination flourished in camaraderie."
— DAN CHIASSON, *NEW YORKER*

"Honest and eloquent . . . Ruhl's attentive and loving communications are met
by increasingly vivid and vulnerable reports. . . . [Ritvo's] prose, rich with
the mischief, directness, and erotic buoyancy that made Max unforgettable
to anyone who met him, effortlessly conveys complex ideas and captures his
inimitable spirit."
— *SLATE*

"I will read more books in my life but I will not love another book more than
this one. I suspect this book has the power to reassure the weary and to instill
faith in anyone who needs it. If they let you bring books when you die, I will
100 percent put this one in the tiny stack that goes with me."
— MARY-LOUISE PARKER, AUTHOR OF *DEAR MR. YOU*

"Revelatory in every way, *Letters from Max* is an unusual, beautiful book
about nothing less than the necessity of art in our lives. Two big-hearted,
big-brained writers have allowed us to eavesdrop on their friendship: jokes
and heartbreaks, admiration, hard work, tender work."
— ELIZABETH MCCRACKEN, AUTHOR OF *BOWLAWAY*

"*Letters from Max* is a sublime journey shared by two brilliant minds. . . . It is
stunning to see that these letters offer so much peace. They read like guided
meditations, lived hymns, the good voices we seek within our own heads."
— *BOMB*

"Immediate comparisons will be made to Rainer Maria Rilke's *Letters to a
Young Poet.* . . . This book is a nuanced look at the evolution of an incredible
talent facing mortality and the mentor, never condescending, who recog-
nizes his gift. Their infectious letters shine with a love of words and beauty."
— *THE OBSERVER*

"I expected the letters between these two artists to be profoundly brilliant
and profoundly heartbreaking. And they are. But what I didn't expect, and
what makes the experience of reading this conversation a sublime one, is
the abiding and generous humor throughout, the element that, as Ritvo
says, 'makes our sadness rhyme with joy.' Resisting any lesson to be found
in Ritvo's impending death, the letters between these two friends instead

enact a deep and instructive compassion and pay ardent attention to what it means to continue to live a life, even one that will end tragically and too soon. In giving the world these breathtaking letters, Ruhl, with humility and humanity, goes far in preserving the legacy of the poet Max Ritvo."

—CARRIE FOUNTAIN, AUTHOR OF *I'M NOT MISSING*

"*Letters from Max* is a story of two brilliant beings unfolding each other's hearts and minds until even death is a gift and listening never ends. I read it once without stopping and read it again and again. Every page is a revelation about the unflinching mysteries of life."

—BETH HENLEY, WINNER OF THE PULITZER PRIZE FOR DRAMA

"It is at once painful and enlightening to eavesdrop on the correspondence between playwright Ruhl and the late poet Ritvo. . . . What emerges from their brilliant, funny, heartbreaking conversations is a frank exploration of human connection, mortality, art, and much more in precious real time. . . . Theirs is a life and death conversation, deftly seasoned with poetry."

—*SHELF AWARENESS*

"A beautiful, grounded, and intensely abbreviated search for meaning . . . Ruhl and Ritvo take the reader deep into some of the most challenging questions we face as human beings. . . . They both express, in numerous ways, that neither of them knows anything for sure but love. The sanguinity of this shared understanding is beautifully tempered by undisguised honesty, necessary humor, and an urgent spiritual playfulness."

—*WORLD LITERATURE TODAY*

"The agile, luminous minds and tender, perceptive hearts of these two writers . . . chart the rare and complex process of two artists coming to truly see and know one another. . . . Both Ritvo and Ruhl hoped their correspondence would bring solace to those facing death or losing loved ones; this intimate gift also rekindles hope in the bright possibility of profound human connections." —*BOOKLIST* (STARRED REVIEW)

"Deeply moving, often heartbreaking . . . A captivating celebration of life and love." —*KIRKUS* (STARRED REVIEW)

"Moving and erudite . . . Devastating and lyrical . . . Ruhl draws a comparison between their correspondence and that between poets Robert Lowell and Elizabeth Bishop, and indeed, with the depth and intelligence displayed, one feels in the presence of literary titans." —*PUBLISHERS WEEKLY*

LETTERS

from

MAX

LETTERS

from

MAX

a poet, a teacher, a friendship

SARAH
RUHL *and*
MAX
RITVO

MILKWEED EDITIONS

© 2018, Text by Sarah Ruhl and Max Ritvo
All rights reserved. Except for brief quotations in critical articles or reviews, no part of this
book may be reproduced in any manner without prior written permission from the publisher:
Milkweed Editions, 1011 Washington Avenue South, Suite 300, Minneapolis, Minnesota 55415.
(800) 520-6455
milkweed.org

First paperback edition, published 2019 by Milkweed Editions
Printed in Canada
Cover design by Mary Austin Speaker
Cover illustration by Mary Austin Speaker
19 20 21 22 23 5 4 3 2 1

978-1-57131-375-1

Milkweed Editions, an independent nonprofit publisher, gratefully acknowledges sustaining
support from the Alan B. Slifka Foundation and its president, Riva Ariella Ritvo-Slifka; the
Ballard Spahr Foundation; *Copper Nickel*; the Jerome Foundation; the McKnight Foundation;
the National Endowment for the Arts; the National Poetry Series; the Target Foundation;
and other generous contributions from foundations, corporations, and individuals. Also, this
activity is made possible by the voters of Minnesota through a Minnesota State Arts Board
Operating Support grant, thanks to a legislative appropriation from the arts and cultural heri-
tage fund. For a full listing of Milkweed Editions supporters, please visit milkweed.org.

Library of Congress Cataloging-in-Publication Data

Names: Ritvo, Max, 1990-2016, author. | Ritvo, Max, 1990-2016,
    Correspondence. Selections. | Ruhl, Sarah, 1974- Correspondence.
    Selections.
Title: Letters from Max : a book of friendship / Mark Rivko and Sarah Ruhl.
Description: Minneapolis, Minnesota : Milkweed Editions, 2018.
Identifiers: LCCN 2018007328 (print) | LCCN 2018016012 (ebook) | ISBN
    9781571319760 (ebook) | ISBN 9781571313690 (hardcover : alk. paper)
Subjects: LCSH: Ritvo, Max, 1990-2016,--Correspondence. | Ruhl, Sarah,
    1974---Correspondence. | Poets, American--20th century--Correspondence. |
    Cancer--Patients--Correspondence. | Women dramatists, American--20th
    century--Correspondence. | Drama teachers--Correspondence.
Classification: LCC PS3618.I8 (ebook) | LCC PS3618.I8 Z48 2018 (print) | DDC
    811/.6--dc23
LC record available at https://lccn.loc.gov/2018007328

Milkweed Editions is committed to ecological stewardship. We strive to align our book
production practices with this principle, and to reduce the impact of our operations in the
environment. We are a member of the Green Press Initiative, a nonprofit coalition of publishers, manufacturers, and authors working to protect the world's endangered forests and
conserve natural resources. *Letters from Max* was printed on acid-free 100% postconsumer-
waste paper by Friesens Corporation.

CONTENTS

Introduction | 1

Part One:
New Haven, 2012–13 | 7

Part Two:
New York, 2013–15 | 69

Part Three:
New York and California, 2015–16 | 117

Part Four:
California, 2016 | 215

Then:
Everywhere. Time Unimportant | 293

Afterword | 311

Acknowledgments | 315

Text and Illustration Credits | 317

A friend is a person with whom I may be sincere. Before him, I may think aloud.

—RALPH WALDO EMERSON

✳

A Greek word, *storge*, denotes a tender care, affection uniting parents and children. Perhaps some teachers feel such a love for their pupils. It is also not impossible that *storge* may be applied to the relationship between a poet and generations of readers to come: underneath the ambition to perfect one's art without hope of being rewarded by contemporaries lurks a magnanimity of gift-offering to posterity.

—CZESLAW MILOSZ
A Book of Luminous Things

✳

At Laguna, when someone dies, you don't "get over it" by forgetting; you "get over it" by *remembering*.

—LESLIE MARMON SILKO
The Delicacy and Strength of Lace

Introduction

Max Ritvo began as my student. I met Max when he was a senior at Yale. This is how he began his application to get into my playwriting workshop:

> Dear Professor Ruhl,
>
> Thanks for reading this application. My name is Max Ritvo—I'm a senior English major in the Creative Writing Concentration. All I want to do is write.

His application said that he was a poet and a comedian, part of an experimental comedy troupe. A poet *and* he's funny? Huh. I reread his application, which had been left to stew in the "no" pile because he'd never written a play before.

And because funny poets are a rare and wonderful species of human being, I moved Max to the "yes" pile, despite his lack of experience writing plays. It is hard to imagine now that Max's application could ever have remained in any other pile—a strange parallel universe in which I never met Max.

✳

Max walked into my first class and it was as though an ancient light bulb hovered over his head, illuminating the room. Skinny to the point of worry, eyes luminous blue and large, even larger under his thick glasses. His eyes (both magnified and magnifying) were especially animated after he'd amused someone, anyone; with a hangdog look, he'd gaze up from behind his spectacles to see if the joke had found a target. His voice: surprisingly booming for so slight a frame. Some rarefied combination of a young Mike Nichols and an old John Keats, he seemed eighty years old and not from this century. *Who is this boy?* I wondered. He seemed to have read everything, from Vedic texts to contemporary poetry, and yet he had the air of a playful child.

The first missive I received from Max in my inbox began like this:

Dear Professor Ruhl,

I am writing because, before shopping period had even begun or I had even realized that this wonderful class existed, I booked tickets for *Einstein on the Beach* at the Brooklyn Academy of Music for this coming Friday.

Little did he know that I had longed to see *Einstein on the Beach*, had tried in fact to get a ticket, but it was sold out. Nothing could have been more delightful to me than a student who had the foresight to book tickets to a difficult and avant-garde theatrical epic. Max went on to apologize and ask permission to miss a class. I told Max that he must go, and I asked him for a short report (no more than five minutes) on the experience of seeing the show. I said maybe he could join us for the first part of class, then hightail it to Brooklyn to hear the great Philip Glass score.

Max wrote back, "Dear Sarah" (it took us two letters to drop the institutional formalities):

> The show starts at seven. I'm worried if I leave later I
> won't have time to properly get from Grand Central to
> eat something! The show is four hours long and I have
> to eat in a really regimented way to keep my weight up
> as a result of the cancer/chemotherapy I had in high
> school—more on that some other time.

I now had part of my answer as to why Max was different from the other students, why life and death seemed to hover near him, why (beyond being a poet) he'd already contemplated the big metaphysical questions, why he was so skinny. Max went on:

> I would really love to take you up on your offer of some
> post-graduating advice. What days are you in New
> Haven, and when would it be convenient for you to be
> a sage for a half hour?

✳

The following week, Max, as promised, delivered an insightful and detailed sermon to the class on Philip Glass and Robert Wilson. He was to have spoken for five minutes—he spoke for about an hour without stopping. (I later learned that a bright young woman in the class was horrified that a man was taking up an hour of her time with a lecture on Philip Glass; she was to become one of his best friends.) In class, Max had boundless enthusiasm. He had highly refined irony without ever being cynical. And if he was aware that his brain made connections faster than many of his peers, he didn't show it; he just seemed happy to be in such good company.

I met with Max after class at the local bookstore-café, Atticus, where we sat at the counter and ate black bean soup. Max ate slowly, with difficulty, and explained that in high school he'd had Ewing's sarcoma, a rare pediatric cancer, and the chemotherapy made his digestion iffy. He explained that he was in remission and slowly finished three spoonfuls of the soup. Then he put his spoon down, and spoke about his dreams of becoming a poet, resting here and there to speak about the trials of love. (A girl was probably plaguing him at the time. A girl was often plaguing him.)

The semester wore on, with more deliciously coined phrases from Max in class (phrases like "theatrical onanism" and "lyric complicity") and more of the same leaves falling on the same gothic campus. Then, in October, another email from Max, addressed to me and to the teaching assistant, Amelia:

Dearest Sarah and Amelia,

I write with sad news. Today was my cancer scanning day and an artifact was discovered in my right chest. We are waiting for more testing and surgical biopsy, but it is possible that this is a recurrence of my cancer. I have

4

every intention of carrying on with my work—I just wanted to forewarn you that there might be some difficulties on the horizon. I can't say how much you've both come to mean to me in my short time learning from you. If nothing else, maybe we'll squeeze a great play out of whatever comes of this.

Gratefully,
Max

The small class and I were heartbroken.

A hurricane was about to arrive in New York City, and Max was about to go into surgery. The conversations Max and I had about art and life took on a new urgency, and our correspondence began in earnest.

Part One:

New Haven, 2012–13.
Or,
"Learn to love everything—the world becomes heaven. . . .
I have a better idea, pass the soap."

Dear Sarah,

I go into surgery in five or six hours. I will miss you—wish me luck as they cut me and fill me with opium and hand down the unappealable verdict!

I will get everything in, perhaps just not in a timely fashion. The idea of my one act is daunting—I might want to do a cancer one act. And I might want to very much not do a cancer one act. I will only have clarity a little later.

In the meantime, I thought you might enjoy a few poems I'm working on: proof of a fecundity, if unsoundness, of mind. Any comments would be deeply appreciated. I'm clinging more and more to my writing as my panic is increasing—and have just not had the concerted span of time necessary to write some of the staged things that are brewing in me.

X

SCAN

Lie flat,
comes the command,
from a voice unsinging;
the voice starts to weep
and I blow it kisses.

Dear Max,

I have been thinking of you and sending you, or trying to send you, powerful wishes of healing.

I loved your poems. You have such an ear, such a mind, such a beautiful singing ear and intellect. Thank you for the gift of them.

I am terribly terribly sorry about what seems to be the news of the artifacts. I am assuming that the fact that you emailed yesterday means that you are out of surgery. That is a comfort, and I hope you are resting and recuperating from the invasion.

I want you to write in any way that makes sense to you this semester.

Max, is there anything I can do to help? Happy to visit the hospital if you're up for visitors, or do you need books or distractions? Or if there's anything I can do for your mom while she is in New York during the hurricane?

We are all rooting for you,
Sarah

Sarah,

I can't tell you how much your note means to me.

I am in my room at home—tomorrow, assuming the hurricane doesn't box me in, I will be back in Sloan's to receive the protocol. I will be penned up there for two or three weeks. Then hopefully the treatment can be transferred to New Haven.

It would be great if you're in New York anyway if you visited at the hospital. That would mean a lot to me. Bring me a book and inscribe it! Reading is good. Writing is about all I have.

Today was mostly breathing exercises and limping and coming off of the opiates, as well as the transfer to home. Strange dreams with lots of focus on skin texture. My uncle has flown in from Israel—he gave me some acupuncture, which unblocked a very preverbal chunk of fear and rage—I felt like I was a prophet channeling my tumor.

Max

That fall I was knee deep in rehearsal for a play of mine called *Dear Elizabeth*, an adaptation I wrote of the letters between Robert Lowell and Elizabeth Bishop, that premiered at Yale Repertory Theater. It is strange now to reflect that just as I met Max, I was thinking keenly about the friendship between two writers, expressed through their letters. Bishop and Lowell found in each other's minds a cure for a solitude particular to writers. When I read their letters for the first time, I found their friendship moving, and desperately wanted to hear their letters out loud. It had not been an easy play to write—I was trying to write while one child was vomiting, one child was screaming, and one child was imploring me to read *Mrs. Piggle-Wiggle* out loud. At the time, my twins—Hope and William—were two years old and my big girl—Anna—was five.

And that was the state of affairs when I met Max; motherhood and writing had me feeling underwater much of the time. Meanwhile, Hurricane Sandy hit, rehearsals for my play were canceled for a week, no trains were running between New York and New Haven. I found myself stuck in New York at the same time Max was stuck at the hospital.

Dear Max,

It certainly feels odd in New York. Thank God you're up-
town and were not at NYU. You must feel a little like Job
stuck in the hospital during a hurricane. Like come on, what
gives? And a hurricane too?

I want to come see you and probably can't get to see you until the subways are more under control. Maybe this weekend
if you are still in hospital then?

In the meantime, I'm supposed to be in rehearsals in New
Haven for my play *Dear Elizabeth* and instead am madly
baking at home (luckily we have power) and creating apart-
ment-wide scavenger hunts to entertain the children.

I will try to think of some books that might entertain you.

Sending all good thoughts,
Sarah

Sarah!

I miss you, and the class. Seeing you this weekend would be wonderful. My mornings are spent in the hospital getting chemo drip and then I'm released to my apartment in the afternoons. It would probably be nice to spare you the childhood chemo ward (which is horrific) and the least functional part of my day, and see you in the afternoon.

I'm midway through the first run of chemo. The side effects seem to be accumulating, but I can talk and walk a little bit, and think clearly if with a marked slowing of pace. I'll send you some of my writing.

I am so lucky to feel your warmth and concern. You are such a specific helpfulness in my life. Don't know what I'd do without you.

Max

I visited Max after that surgery in New York, at his apartment on the Upper East Side, as soon as Hurricane Sandy allowed me to brave the subway. I brought noodle kugel and met his family. Max teased that though I was a Midwestern goy, my kugel passed his beautiful mother's Israeli muster. Max was always good company, even post-surgery. I could tell he was furious if he wasn't well enough to make the people around him laugh. If he was not well enough to make people laugh, he usually told friends not to come by.

I gave him *Dear Elizabeth* to read because he was wrestling with the ethics of quoting someone else's letter in the play he was working on. I thought Max would enjoy reading Lowell and Bishop's whopping fight about the ethics of Lowell using letters from his ex-wife in his book *Dolphin*.

Max was still very much my student—I gave him notes like "Put that speech in iambic pentameter." "Bring in that scene rewritten with a twenty-five percent word reduction." "Write a little song for that moment." I would write him about a scene: "I love how specific and never arbitrary you are." And he would write me about his hopes for a new scene: "I am adamant that something extravagant and silent happen."

Max handed in his play at the end of the semester. It begins at an altar, and also features a scene in which a sick boy goes to get a new tattoo, but at the tattoo parlor, the tattoo artist is something of an analyst, and the boy and the tattoo artist speak in iambic pentameter. The boy says to the tattoo artist:

"So I have brought inside my little pouch,
a little draft of a Hokusai crane."

Max got a tattoo after every surgery. He wanted to make something beautiful out of something painful. They were all birds, modeled after different artists. One was a crane, inscribed on his head, inspired by the Japanese artist Hokusai. In his tattoo parlor play, Max wrote these stage directions:

The tattoo artist finishes, and picks the boy up, very gently like an angel helping another angel. She offers him a compact mirror gently like an angel offering a compact mirror to another angel. He smiles and begins to check it out.

Then the boy says: "It's dope. I really love it in this light."

Dear Max,

It was a delight to see you today; you triumph over portal and charcoal and are great company. I also enjoyed meeting your mom and dad.

I want to invite you to come see my play *Dear Elizabeth* when you're back at Yale, or come see a rehearsal if you can.

Good luck with the move back to New Haven and let me know if there's any way I can be of help. Looks like the matzo ball soup department is covered.

More soon,
Sarah

That long winter, amid chemotherapy and scans, Max worked hard to graduate from Yale. His mother stayed with him in New Haven to help him through chemotherapy.

Not only was Max dealing with mortality and school, he was dealing with all the vagaries of college life. Perhaps my empathy was informed by my own experience of college. My father was diagnosed with cancer in the fall of my freshman year, and I lost him a year later. So college was, for me, a bizarre juxtaposition between my own extreme grief and a private, obsessive attempt to get some wisdom from books and teachers. My teachers at Brown University invited me to their homes, and into their lives, and I think that gave me the strength to remain far from home. I lived for my frequent trips from Providence home to Chicago, and somehow survived the indignities of being twenty, surrounded by many drunk young people who were thinking not at all of mortality.

So I imagined that there was a gulf between Max and the young people who surrounded him, who couldn't quite fathom what he was experiencing. He would write me, asking if we could speak on the phone, saying, "My romantic life is falling apart; I don't really know how to talk to people about my illness in a nondestructive way, or how they're supposed to listen, and you write really wonderful listeners."

Always, always, Max wanted to know what was the best way to listen. Perhaps because I wrote characters who listened to each other, Max suspected that I might be a good listener.

✳

Max came to *Dear Elizabeth* at Yale Repertory Theater. He hugged me afterward, in tears, and said he felt I'd written the play just for him. And though I hadn't met Max when I wrote that play, it did feel somehow that I'd written the play just for him.

※

That winter, we pursued soup. And shared poems.

Max somehow got me to share with him my early poems, written when I was his age. I seldom share my poems with people. Emily Dickinson's envelope poems are to me the height of beauty—unshared, unfinished, written on envelopes—as partial as they are sublime, as hidden as they are revealed.

My plays get consumed by audiences in front of me; the audiences either laugh or don't laugh, clap heartily or not at all; the plays get reviewed well or badly; this was as much vulnerability, I'd decided, as one writer could absorb in one lifetime. The poems were private. I wrote them as gifts for other people—occasion poems, you might say, in the old-fashioned tradition. I wanted desperately to be a poet before I discovered playwriting, but once I wrote plays, I began to think there was a kind of equation for playwrights— indifferent-to-bad poets made good playwrights. The poems were a compost heap for the plays. And if you like your friends, you don't send them compost in the mail.

But Max asked for more poetry, and Max could be very persuasive.

In sharing our poetry with each other, I came to feel less and less Max's "teacher," and more his colleague and friend. I was certainly not the only teacher who had a close working relationship with Max. Max spoke often of the astonishing poet Louise Glück, who mentored him beautifully at Yale and afterward. Max would go on to charm scores of teachers who ended up asking for Max's feedback on their own writing.

That Max turned many of his teachers into colleagues in short order, as fast as you could flip a pancake, was not surprising. The transformation was immediate because it did not take long for a perceptive teacher to see Max as an equal. I was certainly not the only teacher of his to dissolve the formal boundaries between the teacher and the taught. And this reversal was not at all a lack of reverence for his teachers— quite the opposite. He would emphatically introduce me as his Teacher with a capital T long after he was my student at Yale. The transformation of his teachers into fellow writers was more to do with reciprocity.

Max's generosity could not bear to take without giving, could not bear to be read without also reading. Poetry was, to Max, a conversation. He didn't want to chirp his epic songs into an unsinging receptacle. He wanted them to answer back. He wanted a poem to answer a poem. He wanted his writing to beget more writing.

He told me that with the time he had left, all he wanted to do was write poetry. He was applying to graduate school in poetry. He asked me for a recommendation. I said yes.

Dear Sarah,

Your recommendation letters arrived. I am so deeply grateful to you. I nearly cried when I read the letter. Working with you and coming to admire you as much as I have from reading you, watching you, receiving the warmth in your human heart as well your literary heart, I felt a pretty fucking close to miraculous sense of joy to hear that the connection is mutual. You complimented my ear. Nobody ever compliments my ear. Secretly, I am very proud of my ear. Everything in my life, the fabric of my life itself, is dissolving. You are not. Maybe I am not? That's what your letter meant to me.

The cancer is very, very scary right now. It keeps changing the terms of the contract. I wept a lot today in the bathroom. I am now more terrified than ever of going back into chemoland, feeling like the chemo isn't even efficacious. I was starting to get really hopeful about my MFA plans, and the prospect of writing poetry full time. Now I'm scared I might not make it to that stage, or I will end up plugged into some experimental protocol after a semi-botched chemo attempt.

Thank you for your goodness and your kindness.

Max

Dear Max,

If it's poems you want, it's poems you shall have.

As promised, here is one poem I wrote. (Unpublished and largely unread but by my husband who I wrote it for.) How was your reading? I am having socks knitted for you by one Ms. Evelyn Love who lives on Pond Street. Let's make our dinner plan soon.

xoxo,
Sarah

You know what a lee is; I don't.
Behind a stone. No wind. Stop boat. A place.
Behind your back. My body. Stop the air.
Travel by stopping, full stop, just there.

As lee is a small word. Sail easy.
Lee and unlee, light is hot.
Rest here, a while longer on my
belly. A lee, a dry derry, a drought.

August: marsh sounds, marsh looks, a ferry.
Look for other words—lucid, pellucid—
call a mind a pond? Call a pond a mind?
Lucid, penitent mendicants on a pond.

Words for clarity, words for light and heat,
words for charity—words for sleep.

Sarah, I know I'm poetry biased, but this made me shimmer inside. I want to write with this kind of glow, and this kind of penetration/purity (and intelligence) one day. I have read it out loud so many times. I am going to use sounds. I am going to read out loud more, and have words fall back into one another and into one another's arms!

The first stanza . . . makes me want to play peekaboo. I can't even. It's moving—I want to move. I want this miracle in my life. . . . The elisions. The life. Oh God, Sarah, seriously that first stanza I could read a billion times.

I'm excited for socks, and for dinner.

Love,
Max

Oh, Max. Thank you so much. I will keep sending you little poems then. Maybe you will give me the courage to send them out one day. I'm terribly private about them. In some ways, you know, you are my teacher, not the other way around.

Socks and dinner soon! And how was your poetry reading?

All good thoughts sent to you,
Sarah

Dear Sarah,

The reading went fabulously—full of loved ones. I have connected with some other poets and they say they want me to come to Brooklyn to do a reading. Maybe you could come to one! (Some of the other poems were a little deliberately and finicky opaque . . .)

The next day I went to Louise [Glück]'s house and we hashed over some editing I did and some new work. It's basically me shedding portention and allowing the poem to be a humbler thing than I wanted it to be, but still a thing that I can be proud of.

I'm exhausted from the chemo this week, and have spent lots of time fearing the upcoming scans. So many uncertainties. There's talk of a stem cell transplant which would involve even more heinous levels of chemotherapeutic dosing than I've ever experienced. And then I could relapse within two months. I'm bitter, Sarah, I'm bitter and love the world and it won't love me back.

Missing you,
Max

Dearest Max,

I'm so glad your reading went well.

Oh, and on the school of poets who surround you, I say: *resist opacity*. I think at the heart of opacity is fear. I think ultimately it was a similar experience I had when I was your age that made me wander away from poetry; that is to say, the poetry that was privileged at college was opaque and academic and my transparency was hugely embarrassing.

I'm going to save your poem for my Amtrak ride to New Haven today. And I'll send you another poem soon. But for today, a song!

I hope you don't have to go through the labor of a stem cell transplant. I want everything good for you. Love, health, poetry.

Okay, *Dora* is almost over on the television, I must go attend to the twins.

xo,
Sarah

The song I sent him was from *Melancholy Play: a chamber musical*. It goes like this, set to music:

TILLY:

Do you ever have the feeling, when you wake up in the morning, that you're in love but you don't know with what?

It's this feeling—
that you want to love strangers,
that you want to kiss the man at the post-office,
or the woman at the dry-cleaners—
you want to wrap your arms around life, life itself
but you can't
and this feeling wells up
and there is nowhere to put this
great happiness—
and you're floating—and then you're falling—
and then you have to lie down on the couch.

FRANCES: *(simultaneously)*   JOAN:
Are you still in therapy Tilly?   I know what you mean.

Sarah:

A proper note.

Melancholy Play in this song form is confusing and beautiful—the bricolage of musical intonations gives it a dizzy interpersonal body. It's like how I imagine people engaged with opera when it was part of daily life. (I can't follow operas the way I imagine they deserve to be followed, and this makes me feel like I get an opera-like experience—free from the overconventionalization of musicals but complicated in a register I can intuitively relate to.) Please send me more, and more poems. (Still love your poems best.)

The stomach holds up today, the flu seems to be in check. I don't even want to talk about my physical health if I'm able to focus on anything else for two seconds in a row. I sense a wall from D. and I can't blame her, I haven't spoken to her in years, and all of a sudden I'm barging very suddenly and cancerily into her presence. We had a meal where she seemed to be obliging me. She called me "dude" at one point. Sarah, can you imagine anyone referring to me as "dude"? Urgh.

I am writing fairly good poems. More exciting has been the editing. Opacity is fear. I'm editing with that in mind. I'm noticing the poems are humbler than I thought they were, but

that they have a sincere wit and imagination that is just fine on
its own, even if I can't live up to the crazily inflated diction of
a Stevens. Opacity is fear. Embrace my voice and mind.

Love,
Max

Dear Sarah,

A big chunk of our conversing today ended up in a very strange poem-thing. Wanted to share with you, since you are a prime mover in the poem.

I know this is still a first draft and I would love your input.

It was so much fun seeing you today—thank you for being you.

I will write more when it's not the middle of the night after trying to write a poem all night.

Love,
Max

LISTENING, SPEAKING, AND BREATHING

I.

Pianos are told to repeat
the grieving tones of a bird.

How does the bird focus?
How does the piano focus, in turn?

II.

Wind is a force through air.
Air is the soft gilding powder of the chest.

The soft gilding powder that departs
into the shaking mural of the blood.

III.

Sense is not the same as essence.
Essence is entangled with the sliver of my voice.

Life might be very small victories and meanings.
Is saying "joy" a joyous thing, in and of itself?

IV.

Even if the tune seats the sense for an instant,
like a cloud through which blue is visible.

The red stripe of piping beef circling down
obnoxiously murmurs at death till it hushes.

V.

I have never listened, alone.
Always a guide, a fabric of love and need, absorbing in the ear.

Even the unlistening God
listens more than your own life.

VI.

Love comes from the mouth or in the heart
open on both ends, a craggy tunnel.

The impure love I make is all I know,
but its contents insist that there are others to make it.

VII.

To listen alone might find me
for once assured of a meaning in me.

Distraction, love, companion of narration,
you are not silence.

VIII.

In case of silence, could I cope?
The slender rod of my sense

white and pocked and feathered,
draws a triangle of fire in pure salt:

IX.

This shape is what is required to denote nothing more than me:
no unessential tissues, leaves, ponds, or songs.

I am boiling tar, transformed, or a thing in tar,
a thrill of heat or still a bone.

X.

If I am still an object,
then we'll know that, won't we?

I hope then, you'll talk to me,
and I promise I'll make sense of you.

Dear Max,

It is gorgeous and sublime.

That is my input.

My other input is that the answer to the question posed in your poem is always yes—

the eternal yes that poets sing about,

the yes of the poet's immortality.

xo,
Sarah

I have very little memory of that winter or spring. I was teaching graduate student playwrights that semester at Yale. I was also checking my children's temperatures often, as they always seemed to have a cold. I was writing microessays because I felt incapable of writing a play while I was constantly checking my children's temperatures. When the pediatrician saw me, she started to laugh, because I seemed to arrive at her doorstep every other day with one of my three children. I don't know if my friendship with Max felt like an extension of my mothering, or a release from it, or both.

That March, I received a group missive from Max to his circle of friends updating us on his current condition:

> Bleak news, though no immediate death sentence
> impending. My tumors remain unchanged, despite the
> new chemo. My lungs have been too irradiated due to
> my first cancer for a second attempt. The dosage would
> be too low to guarantee a response, and too high to not
> risk killing my lung tissue. Surgery also doesn't seem
> to be a likely option given the subcentimeter size of
> my tumors, their deep enjambment in my lungs, and
> the slipperiness of Ewing's cells. Surgery is also a little
> irrelevant as there are certainly microtumors saturat-
> ing my lungs and perhaps the rest of my bloodstream.
> Systemic treatments are the only things that would give

me a long-term chance of remission. And it doesn't look like the systemic therapies (chemo) are doing what they ought.

It is more likely that I will embark upon a clinical trial, hoping that an experimental vaccine therapy treatment at the NIH will be able to give me a clean scan.

These trials are trials because they are promising, and they are trials because they are not proven science. I will be on the periphery of medicine. Empiricists (like Dad) love the sentiment that man's reach should always exceed his grasp. My body is being fanned and fumbled by the gloved fingertips. I hope they can get a grip on me, but I can't say the odds are very good.

Should the trial fail, my tumors will probably start growing again very quickly. We will try to find another trial, or we will consider nursing more chemo. I honestly can't tell you.

That spring, Max underwent chemotherapy while trying to graduate from Yale. He had lung surgery at Sloan Kettering. I visited him after, in New York. We took a walk around the block. We took a selfie. Here it is:

I always liked that picture. I have Bell's palsy, so half of my face is crooked when I smile. But in this picture half of my face is cut off, so I look legitimately happy. Funny that Max and I both look happy when he was in so much pain.

Dear Sarah:

I am very sad—Good Friday closed my New Haven chemo hospital and I will have to trek up to New York for Friday, Saturday, Sunday. Will you be in New York any of those days? I am waiting for the arrival of the book I wanted to give you.

You are the best gift to have delivered in person. I have been struggling to adjust to jet lag and chemo.

I have good news: I got into the Columbia MFA! Whee!

My mother has even discussed the prospect of me doing chemo alone in New York and giving me some salvaged autonomy even if I'm on these demon drugs.

Dear Max,

Hooray about Columbia!!!

All the kiddos are sick with high fevers. So we've been hanging out watching *Scooby-Doo*. Here's an old poem for you.

xo,
Sarah

I wanted music   yes

but I also wanted the music

of every day things

a plate   an arm   some dirt   a chair

how a plant is related to a window

how a window is related to a chair

small words with purpose

correspondences

of every day things

the music of objects

one day ending

not tracking for posterity

but loosening like a fig

Sarah dear,

The "small words with purpose" of your last poem have stuck in me. I think it goes along with the meditation I ought to be doing. That whole poem does. And maybe on a different level is a way to get away from some of the aggrandizing camp in my own work.

Will you be around come graduation? Could we have a phone call soon—I would like to talk with you and hear your wisdom on things that have been rotating around my mind. The use of apolitical art. Camp and its relationship to my work. Building a coherent understanding of my personality. Developing a healthier relationship with consistency in the way my mind applies itself.

Love,
Max

Max:

The only way I can think of to develop a healthier relationship with the way the mind applies itself are:

1) writing routines
   and
2) meditation

Camp . . . longer conversation.

Building a coherent understanding of your personality . . .
maybe there is no need?

Live your way into the questions (in Rilkean fashion).

Or back to:

2) meditate . . .

Also I wish I were there to watch you march at graduation!

You deserve a triumphant graduation, and great joy!

I just finished a draft of my play about reincarnation and I
wanted to send it to you for your reading pleasure.

See you on Tuesday and talk soon.

xo,
Sarah

The play I sent Max was called *The Oldest Boy*. It is about a couple (a Tibetan man, and an American woman) who are told that their child is the reincarnation of a high Buddhist lama (or teacher), and that, according to tradition, they must give their child to be educated from an early age at a monastery in India. They spend the play trying to figure out what to do, how to let their boy go.

I thought of Max a good deal while writing the play. Even the title in some ways refers to Max—because I always found him to be the oldest youngest person. In the acknowledgments, I thank him for his teachings. The play is ultimately about teachers and students, and the cyclical transmissions that pass between them.

In traditional Tibetan Buddhism, after a high lama dies, his student actually looks for the teacher as a reincarnated child. Once the child is found, the student becomes the teacher of his old teacher. I read a lot of books while doing research for the play, and the books changed me. While reincarnation seemed like a fairy tale before my reading a suitcase full of books, I came to feel it as a real possibility, as likely as any other version of the afterlife that I'd been exposed to—the heaven of my Catholic childhood, or the void of my atheist teens.

Sarah,

First of all, thank you for the play: now I know what to do with my self for the next few days. My God. Sarah. I cannot begin to tell you how moved I am by your acknowledgment. No words.

I miss you. I owe you a call: it surfaces in my mind every day but I'm usually only lucid enough to follow through with something like that at night, and you're a mom who needs her sleep. I will try to steal a reasonable hour from myself at which to call you.

Crising on a lot of fronts. Chemo over: no change in tumors. This means—what the hell is going to happen to me with this experimental cocktail they're going to inject into me? General feelings of anxiety have disconnected me a lot from art: starting to worry that my poetry work is indulgent and insulated. I've been living with my parents all summer and all of last year: I'm terrified of getting back on the horse of living alone, especially considering how supportive my parents have been emotionally and psychologically. I also really really want to live alone. I don't think I'm capable of functioning properly without a Not-Mom-Woman in my life. ("Not-Mom-Woman" is a blues hit, by the by.) This isn't a good thing, but it's a fact. There are some potential romantic prospects, one of which makes me really hopeful—but

I don't want to *need* a Not-Mom-Woman. I want to just WANT a Not-Mom-Woman.

P.S. "I always thought I hated washing dishes. But it's nice to just dry a dish in the rain."

So. Beautiful. A universe of wetness surrounding a home of dryness.

The scene that Max refers to is one in which the American woman and Tibetan man fall in love very suddenly while washing dishes together:

MOTHER:
I want to help you. I want to wash the dishes with you. I—

FATHER:
You do?

MOTHER:
Yes.

FATHER:
Well, all right. Then I can't charge you for your meal.

MOTHER:
Oh, that's all right.

FATHER:
I insist.

MOTHER: (*as in now our relations have entirely changed*)
Then I'm no longer a customer.

FATHER:
No.

MOTHER:

We put our arms into soapy warm water.

FATHER:

We didn't talk.

MOTHER:

We washed dish after dish.

FATHER:

Well, I washed.

MOTHER:

I dried.

FATHER:

I like washing.

MOTHER:

I like drying.

They wash dishes for a while.
These might be real dishes, or imaginary.
In any case, the audience's attention slows
as they experience the feeling, real or imagined,
of soap and water.

FATHER:
Then she said:

MOTHER:
I always thought I hated washing dishes. But it's nice to just dry a dish in the rain.

Oh, thank you so much, Max, for your kind words.

I am so sorry that the chemo hasn't appeared to shrink the tumors yet. That must be very hard for you, and to contemplate the experimental therapy. When would the experimental therapy happen?

On other fronts:

Don't worry if your poetry feels insulated or indulgent. Poetry by nature is insulated and indulgent, from Sappho to Whitman to Strand to Dickinson. Only some small degree of emotional restraint keeps it from being indulgent, and some small degree of sharing it with others keeps it from being insulated.

Also don't worry if you're not writing. You have plenty to contend with in the moment, and the writing will come when it needs to.

The Not-Mom-Woman made me laugh. I would say: living alone is overrated. Personally, I hate it. I only like living alone from 9:00 a.m. to 5:00 p.m. At 5:00 p.m. I'm very happy to have a mom around, or a mom substitute.

Let's find a way to connect this summer when we are all in California. Our house will have a trampoline in the backyard.

Give my regards to your mom.

xo,
Sarah

P.S. I just saw I spelled your name wrong in my acknowledgments! The *k* is forever banished!

Sarah,

That is all very good advice, and calmed me down a little.

It might be okay to need somebody.

Your play continues to ripple in me. Attached find a poem stirred up by it. I don't think my poem is in a finished state and would love your criticism.

REFUGE
For Sarah

Rain falls on the house.
My mother dries dishes
in the dark house in the rain.

"I'm your little dish,"
I tell her, even though I ought to be a man.

"You're a big dish."

"You mean I'm very wet."

I haven't seen much,
and don't see much:
The jungle of my short life is one row of white straight naked
    trees.
The vines are white and fall apart in my hands,
as if dissolved under the tongue.
Every living thing is screaming dust.

To imagine a heaven is to admit
there are things in this
world you think you could never bring yourself to love,
even given an unlimited number of attempts.

"Learn to love everything—the world becomes heaven."

"That sounds hard: I have a better idea, pass the soap."

I tell you now,
unhappily knitted to bravery,
that all you must do
is hate yourself
round and round,
hand in hand, foaming mouth open,
rainbow bubbles dashing open.

Hate yourself more
than any other thing:
you have made heaven.

Heaven's Proverb:
When your milk Finally spills,
may it feed the toxic white slug
impaled by the heel
of the tyrant's loose sandal.

Dearest Max,

I love your poem. Thank you so much for writing it, and for sharing it with me.

I am very honored to have a Max poem dedicated to me, you know. I love it.

I wasn't sure about the last stanza, somehow it reminded me of T. S. Eliot as a gesture towards something oracular or multivocal in italics, and something about your poem was more intimate. I suppose I wondered if the idea of hating yourself to create heaven needed a rebuttal, or another artic- ulation, rather than moving into the abstract at the very end.

Something about the ordinary scene of washing dishes with one's mother . . . it's very beautiful, Max.

With your round of chemo done are you still immunosup- pressed? Wonder if you'd like to see the kids or if they would still be too germy. Could be fun to go to the Ferris wheel in Santa Monica or something. Or Tony's old kid playground.

I wrote a poem the other day that reminds me slightly of some of the questions you are posing. It's funny how mundane the impulse for a poem can be. In my case, I got a bad burn making cheesy grits, of all things! Pathetic kitchen accident!

Consider the beauty of a horse.
Consider the beauty of a foot.

Then:

Consider a blister. From a burn.
How it covers the skin while it heals.

Consider its ugliness and how it
Hides the promise of new skin.

Then:

Consider the fact of considering.
Considerate children, and considerate beasts.

And then:
How can one want to leave this earth?

With its horses, feet, ugliness, and thought—
all of its terrible regeneration?

Dear Sarah,

More on your poem in a little bit. I want to ask you about
your process—you produce things that are so alive and flex-
ible and bamboo-like.

Dear Max,

I don't know much about my process except that it involves tea.

Love,
Sarah

Max, at this point, had left New Haven, and was shuttling between his mother's home in Los Angeles and treatments in New York at Memorial Sloan Kettering.

Summers often have me visiting my in-laws in Los Angeles. On my family trip to California that summer, we all went to have sushi in the Valley. My husband, Tony; my three kids; Max; and me. Max joked that the only way to get him to drive to the Valley was to see my family.

My oldest daughter, Anna, who was about seven at the time, adored Max. Children were drawn to Max because he was playful and empathetic, and didn't care about grown-up social mores.

At lunch, Max looked very skinny. Frightened. We did not go to a Ferris wheel. It seemed like too much.

I remember that summer my twins were three years old. It was the summer they learned to swim.

Dear Max,

I was so happy to see you. Even though the happiness was tempered by what you're going through.

I wrote a poem for you while I was filling the bathtub up with water tonight and when I finished the water had almost overflowed but didn't. It is attached. (The poem, not the bathwater.)

Take heart, take courage, you're very brave.

xo,
Sarah

FOR MAX
With thanks to Maurice Sendak

Death no wild thing
and you a boy,
Max.

One night in your room
(or body)
a forest grew

and the walls
(or cells) became
transparent

because brightness
invites
transparency, I guess.

Then a little boat
to hospital smells.
Doctors called

the forest cancer,
not obscuring leaves.
and you a boy.

You say:

"Why can't people use the word
courage?

instead of something
vulgar and idiomatic
about manhood?"

Courage, I say,
is you,
Max.

In your wild suit
your small boat
and terrible forest

a man overnight
no boy
could ever scale those walls.

You come home
and dinner is waiting,
still waiting, I hope, still warm.

*

And today my small boy
learned to swim.
He said: the water held me, Mama.
It held me.

Speechless.

Love,
Max

Dear Max,

I hope it was not too intrusive.

Speechless can mean one of two things . . . but I trust you divined my intention.

I'm thinking of you as you go into a difficult week.

Just back from thirty-six hours in Disneyland.

Oy.

Tony sends his best and enjoyed meeting you.

Please put us on your list to let us know how the surgery went, even if it's a one-sentence email.

xoxo,
Sarah

No no no! Speechless only in the direction that it is one of the more moving things to happen to me in a while. You discern me, honor me—I just can't . . .—just have to hold the poem up.

Disneyland is very disorienting, isn't it?

I loved meeting your family, all of your children have a kind of calm joy in them that I think you put there. Or maybe Tony. Tony's a doll.

Hell starts on Monday: it'll be three days of pretty constant scanning (and I'm a little afraid of MRI machines) and that'll transition immediately into surgery. Then I'll get to rest and probably lose some weight.

X
Max

Thank you, dear Max. I'm very glad you liked it.

I'm a little afraid of MRI machines too. I don't know why they haven't figured out how to make them more pleasant. If we can put a man on the moon . . .

Okay, thinking of you, sending you all good thoughts . . .

(When I went into labor, my mantra was from *The Little Engine That Could*, "I think I can, I think I can, I think I can . . .")

xoxo,
Sarah

Part Two:

New York, 2013–15.
Or,
"Where to get a good pancake in this dump of a city?"

That fall, Max moved to New York and entered Columbia's MFA program in poetry. He wrote poems like water while undergoing chemotherapy.

Our letters now take on the familiar quality of spontaneous logistical wrangling because we saw each other more often—they are more in the vein of:

From me: "I know you like Halloween. We are having a Halloween party if you want to hang out with kids and see spooky movies." And from Max: "OooOOO Halloween party." Then small missives about my kids: "Spent Halloween with my William and his best pal Annabel, both dressed as Peter Pan, shouting: 'Pixie dust away!' And running down the street." There would be invitations, like "Do you want tickets to my play?" And from Max: "Read a poem with me at my poetry reading on Thirteenth Street?" Or, from me: "Want to eat this weird mushroom soup that is supposed to help with lung cancer? I'll go to Chinatown and buy the mushrooms and cook it." Or: "Send me poems! I'm driving around in a minivan with three kids so need poems like water." Or, from Max: "What is a hinky-pinky for Infinite-Rainbow Guitar Pick?" "Spectrum Plectrum." (Hinky-Pinky is a rhyming game I played when I was little.) Or, quite often, from me: "The kids all have strep, I have to reschedule."

I was busy, in and out of rehearsals for various projects. Conversations with Max were more often in real time over a meal and not in letters. They went something like this, over a slice of pizza:

SARAH:

How did it go to read your poetry out loud last night?

MAX:

It was good, it was nice, it was good of them to ask me. One poet read a poem and I said, "It's funny, I can't quite hear what you're trying to get across because of the static in your poem." And she said, "I'm not trying to get anything across, I don't want you to get anything."

SARAH:

I think that is sad.

MAX:

Yes, it is sad. She is trying to make language revert in on itself so it doesn't communicate anything. Wittgenstein said the only thing that is left is silence and I think what he left out is that the only thing left is love.

SARAH:

Do you think love is silence?

MAX:

No, I don't think so, I think love is relational and I think to understand the concept of love we always understand the idea that the person we love is trying to love us, so we understand intention. So I think there is this relational pocket of love that Wittgenstein is missing.

SARAH:

Like if you dropped Martin Buber's *I-Thou* inside post-modernism—

MAX:

Yes—but I don't know if you can put Buber inside of Wittgenstein.

SARAH:

When I was your age I walked into my professor's office and said, "I don't believe in postmodernism or deconstruction," and she said, "Hmm, what all have you read about it?" and I said, "Hmm, maybe one book or two." Terrible. Arrogant. But I still don't believe in postmodernism.

MAX:

You don't?

SARAH:

Do you?

MAX:

I do! Postmodernism devours everything, it eats everything, it acknowledges the void—

SARAH:

It has an appetite but no stomach!

MAX:

Yes, true—but it is the digestion of the fox and not the hedgehog—it can be playful and loving—for example, it can say, here is a coin from behind my ear, here is a pine cone from behind my ear, not HERE IS A DIALECTIC—

SARAH:

Okay, so it's a victory of smallness against self-importance—

MAX:

Yes—

SARAH:

—but it's so self-important!

MAX:

It can be.

SARAH:

You're saying it's against the totalizing impulse, it's against Casaubon's key to all the mysteries in *Middlemarch*.

MAX:

I haven't read *Middlemarch*, I'm illiterate.

SARAH:

You're hardly illiterate. My friend thought *Middlemarch* was about bunnies.

MAX:

That's *Watership Down*, yes?

SARAH:

Anyway, I think the vision of postmodernism you describe is a new thing, it's to be invented, it's not postmodernism because it's small and humble and loving, it could be called "loving postmodernism" or something—LPM—

MAX:

Yes, LPM—what is LPM?

SARAH:

It's small incursions of meaning into the void—it has to do with smallness—

MAX:

Yes, and with luminous priorities—

SARAH:

Except I don't even want postmodernism in the title because it only defines itself in the negative up against modernism, and I find that inherently nihilistic—

MAX:

It all goes back to the Holocaust and how can we deal with the void and still be a joyous mammal, what can we affirm in the face of the void—

SARAH:

Yes, but postmodernism is not affirmative, and the problem is that Heidegger and his cronies were Nazi sympathizers so they can void out history and that's very convenient.

MAX:

But how do we deal with the void and meaninglessness? My two favorite songs are Nat King Cole's "Smile" as in "smile while your heart's breaking" and "Girls Just Want to Have Fun."

SARAH:

Do you think "Girls Just Want to Have Fun" is a sad song or a happy song?

MAX:

Exactly.

✳

Sometimes Max would text me to distract me from nervousness before I gave a public reading (I am a reluctant public speaker) or to enliven my commute to New Haven. These dialogues would go something like this:

SARAH:

I'm on the Amtrak quiet car, it's like my fairy godmother.

MAX:

Is it godmotherish because it transforms into a magically civilized place? Maybe death is an Amtrak quiet car, then we'd both be right in a way.

SARAH:

Yes. But would we know anyone on the car? And who is the conductor?

MAX:

No, I think you don't know anyone, but there are familiar dinner rolls.

SARAH:

That sounds sad. Are there books?

MAX:

And the conductor is a reticent beautiful Steve Jobs.

SARAH:

That made me laugh.

MAX:

Good.
I think when you die, you are a book so you can't read any other books. Give me some brutal feedback on my new poem; it's new so I'm afraid it isn't any good.

SARAH:

Because I'm so brutal.

MAX:

You're not brutal.

SARAH:

You haven't seen me play ping-pong.

MAX:

Good Lord your dark side.

＊

At my forty-first birthday party at Risotteria Melotti in the East Village, there was a large group of friends and family. Max came and we played the Noel Coward adverb game. It's a game in which one person has to leave the room and the others decide on an adverb they will act out and have that person guess. Max had us all in stitches. Max gave me a tea mug with two fish on it. There was a lot of jollity that year. Max's illness seemed at an arm's length.

We sometimes had lunches on the Upper East Side. I would joke that the only good reasons to come to the Upper East Side from Brooklyn were biopsies, getting highlights, or lunch with Max. I sometimes wrote at the New York Society Library, not far from Max's apartment. I would bury my nose in those old stacks until I disappeared enough to write a play. And sometimes I would emerge into the light and have lunch with Max.

Dear Max,

A little poem for you that I wrote:

LUNCH WITH MAX ON THE UPPER EAST SIDE

1.

The skinny women on the upper east side
have eaten too many salads and
have come to resemble their own salads.
Dry and brittle, they push kale around on their plates.
They need some cooked food, and quick.

You, a young man, also skinny,
push the food around on your plate—
but it's warm and has the flavor of the
poison medicine doctors give you.

2.

The wildness of youth
and the wildness of death—
too much to bear, so close together.
A big why called to God over ageless time . . .

Some loop closed by old age,
the droop of an old man's head
conferring a measure of acceptance,
head already looking at the ground, thinking:
when will a hole open up
and I'll fall into it?

3.

We talk of Madame Bovary and whether her
emotions are banal and whether the doctor's are really *not* banal
and whether emotions can ever even *be* banal
or if they only *seem* banal in art.

Health does not belong to literature.
I wish it did.

Max is a poet.
Max is a poem.

We all become poems
in the end.

Dear Sarah,

I'm gonna cry. I feel like I have a toehold in the world through this poem.

That fall, big news: Max reconnected with a woman he'd known as a teenager, Victoria. She had a luminous smile, was working on a PhD in neuropsychology, and painted beautifully. They fell in love.

I invited the two of them to come see my play *Stage Kiss*. I also sent Max one of the songs I made up for the play as I was always proud to show Max new rhymes, this one of "ethereal" with "cereal." He rejoindered that I was a marimba, and that he and Victoria would happily come see the play.

Dear Max,

I loved seeing you after *Stage Kiss* and meeting the wonderful Victoria. You both brought me great joy and the feeling that the play had been received!

My favorite Sarah,

Victoria and I can't stop talking about the play. I hope to one day die as loved as a quiet number.

What's your schedule like this coming week? I would love to see you and catch up. I'd also like writing advice—these prose poems (that you suggested might be monologues) keep accumulating. I think I might have some sort of a play on my hands. That would be very exciting for me. I know you started in poetry and ended in playwriting, and I'm . . . well . . . much more engaged by what I'm writing now than by all the poems about dead fawns and eating negative space that seem to be what everyone in poetry wants to do. (Unless they want to write arcane language poet crossword puzzles, which has even less of a pull . . .)

I'm not writing plays. It's sort of cross-genre. . . . Oh! And there's another piece I'm thinking about—you know how operas used to rely on little printed libretto summaries and you just sort of had to watch what's going on? I want to write a really detailed libretto for one extremely small action—something like someone smooshing someone else's face, or two people crossing each other and then walking into a wall.

Love,
Max

In April, Max wrote me that his dear friend Melissa had died. She was a talented painter whom he'd met in the pediatric cancer wards, and she also had Ewing's sarcoma. They fought for years as comrades. Her death was a shattering blow to Max, not only for the loss of presence, but because it was a cruel reminder of how Ewing's sarcoma takes people—and in this case a brilliant artist and intimate—far too early.

Max finished writing a chapbook and many of the poems were for and about Melissa. He sent it to me with a small, self-deprecating note: "And here's the little poetry chapbook. It's about my dear Melissa who passed away, my cancer, my love life. The usual suspects."

The "little poetry chapbook" was *Aeons*, which would go on to win an important prize (the Poetry Society of America Chapbook Fellowship), selected by the poet Jean Valentine, leading to publication.

Dearest Max,

I just got to Santa Barbara. Anna woke me up for breakfast and went back to bed. I managed to read three of your gorgeous poems before they got up again. The minimalism, humor, and wisdom in those first three poems . . . I am specially moved by "Receding."

> There is a deeper wholeness than life
> and its white tunnel of projects:
> It is being forgiven
> when you have done nothing.

I can't wait to read all of them. Your writing, I think, is leaping and bounding; I'm so glad you went straight to the MFA program—I think you are finding all kinds of distillatory revelations. Thanks for sharing.

The light here is soft and expansive. I have to pour Chex into a bowl for a child. Then I will write down all my favorite lines from your book.

xoxo,
Sarah

P.S. My favorite lines from your book:

"Rich people are all
desperate to martyr
something other than their own bodies."

"In this world, everything is a miracle:
The rupture of every cell is an unpatterned caprice
adored by a doddering God.
Every drop of explosive water is a young genius
curing the throat into life.

"When he says anything that hurts me,
and I let him know,
father says, *just a joke*."

"Lyric complicity for one . . .
the lullaby sung to another lullaby."

"We call it snow
when the parts of God,

"too small to bear, contest our bodies
for the possession of our smallest sensations.

"This snow brings suffering to the only thing small enough
to have lived peaceably next to suffering."

Dear Sarah,

I love your chapbook selections (and I'm honored that I merit favorites!). You picked out some of my favorite moments too . . . ! "Distilled" is a good word—and I think it comes from a much more severe editing process where I'm stripping away everything that's not remarkable. A kind of robust minimalism.

How is your writing going? Anything amazing? Everything amazing as per usual?

I got official word from the Poetry Society just a few hours ago that the chapbook will be published. You're in the acknowledgments if that's okay with you.

Dearest Max,

I'm working on a play about Peter Pan and my mother. Do you have time to read it?

I'm having trouble with the transition to Neverland. I'll attach it. I'd be grateful for any thoughts at all that you might have.

Yes, robust minimalism! I love that phrase and that aspiration.

Hooray hooray on your chapbook!!! And I'm very honored to be in your acknowledgments. Can't wait to see it in print.

Love,
Sarah

Dear Sarah,

Gonna need some time to let this sink in.

Your dialogue surface and staging can be this ritualistic plainness, and then this glossy-playful-Nozze-di-Figaro-Tolstoy-Lightning-Fast-Effervescent-Copious-Floridity, and then so lovingly and interpersonally textured with information (agon, agora/big kids table/Monica Lewinsky) in such sharp succession. I haven't read anything that manages to make the people do so much and be so beyond people and yet so *people* in such a short and playful little space. I have no idea how it coheres, but I don't feel a transition occurring at any moment (excepting between acts).

I have been thinking a lot about how I sort of imagine this bias of a calm mind being able to do more rhetorically—whenever you get too caught up in emotion you get urgent, sincere, bathetic—you lose the ability to be playful and you're just so much more open to trying out new sentences and bringing in fresh ideas when you're playful. This strikes me as a weird hiccup in Shakespeare, where he obviously had to think really long and hard to make Hamlet say something super "real" and beautiful and interesting, when it's much more likely that, on the spot, Hamlet would've just been like, "Fuck you, Polonius, you're such a douche." But this play is so playful and so agile and organic and still has so much depth. THIS is a kind of "realness" I can get behind! It's urgent and playful. It's sincere and silly even when it's in such deep pain that it shouldn't be silly anymore: and it still retains its sincerity. Maybe urgency and playfulness don't have to be opposed to one another. There can be lethal playfulness (not only in the words but in the ideas: Morphine and Pixie Dust . . . the slaughter of death, and the resurrection of death once he's willing to take off his pretend scythe). And the lethality isn't that serious after all, even though it's the entire world.

And fuck, Sarah: six characters on stage constantly, and I never have to check back to see who is speaking, or forget that someone is on stage? Within the first five pages I had a visual picture of every person who was speaking—and they were all denoted by numbers. Why the fuck are all these people so memorable and how can they still function as a hive mind?

I need to talk to you about this other book I'm reading: Peter Pan and shadow-sewing and renaming and recasting Death are all very relevant to the Vedic Indus River Valley civilization, which has been shaping my poetry recently.

Knowing you is one of the best things that can happen to a mammal in 2014.

Dear Genius Max,

Thank you so much for your close reading of my play and your response. It delights me. Your mind, your mind! How lucky my play is to be in contact with your mind!

I am on Cape Cod right now and the kids are reading *Harold and the Purple Crayon* and overwatering the flowers. I must attend to them but I will write more response to your response very soon when I return to Brooklyn.

I miss you! Let's have a big lunch or dinner soon. It would be fun to have a double date when Victoria is in town. Tony and I could take you both out. We could get a sitter.

xoxo,
Sarah

That week, I got a message on my phone from Max saying that there was a new tumor in his lung and they had to go in and take it out.

The scans that he'd hoped would be "no big deal" were, in fact, harrowing. His voice sounded scared and drawn. I called back but his voicemail was full.

Max had surgery the following month at the NIH. His mother told me that the surgery was on Yom Kippur, and that Max left a note to thank the doctor for getting him out of services.

I visited Max postsurgery in New York. His lungs hurt terribly when he laughed or sneezed. We walked slowly around a three-block radius near his apartment, which in-cluded Sloan Kettering, where Max had spent much time. Oddly, a man walked past us carrying two puppets. One puppet was a skeleton. Max said he felt like a skeleton, and somehow the dark omen made us laugh.

Dear Max,

I loved seeing you. Somehow you always cheer me up, even though you yourself are going through so much. I read your poems on the subway and loved them. So many gorgeous lines—I'll circle them and write them down. Thank you for sharing them.

How are you recovering?

A question—would you like to see *The Oldest Boy* sometime with Victoria? Might I procure you tickets?

Also, I read *Dream Songs* because you recommended them. I was wrestling with not liking him! So I wrote you a poem with a rhyme scheme like Dr. Seuss in honor of wrestling with John Berryman. Or maybe the rhyme scheme is more like the children's book *Madeline*. With my pathetic love of rhyme maybe I should turn to children's books.

Okay, I'm off to rehearsal. Hope you are feeling well. No sneezing!

Love,
Sarah

SOME OLD-FASHIONED RHYMES FOR MAX

1.

Max don't die.
We still have to argue
you and I
about John Berryman
whom you like
and of whom I'd wish
more wisdom
and less intelligence.

2.

How are you feeling,
I ask on the phone.
Terminal, you say.

Laughter makes
us less alone.

3.

We take a walk around the block
to open up your lungs
and talk.

We pass Yew Tree Antiques Store
then two puppets and what's more
the puppets are skeletons and are
playing banjos, four.

4.

It hurts when you sneeze
and on your torso there is a scar,
which you show me —
oh bright star.

Sarah:

Your poem is so funny and so moving and so how I feel about you! The rhymes are amaZing, especially with the skeleton!

I am holding up okay. Little steps. I went to a restaurant for dinner! I ate pizza in public! OooOoOOOOo

I WOULD LOVE TO SEE *THE OLDEST BOY* WITH VICTORIA!!!

How are you?
I love you!
We are two,
A two-person crew,
I play the kazoo
Sarah plays the didgeridoo

Max

Dear Max,

I love the two-person-crew stanza! Thank you!

So glad you are doing well and doing things like eating pizza in public. There is something about eating pizza outside that is a sign of real beneficent normalcy.

When do you and Victoria want to come to the play? I was wondering if later in the run was better in terms of immunity and crowds?

Had the first preview last night. First previews in New York are completely overwhelming and one wants to change a million things immediately. Yesterday in a panic I simply spent time alone with my books. I literally rearranged my bookshelf and dusted them.

I'm very glad to hear from you and to hear you are on the upswing. I'm sorry you have the stress of scans coming up.

I thought of you yesterday. I was getting patronizing notes from a producer on the phone so I started reading Wallace Stevens while he was talking.

Love,
Sarah

P.S. have you read Edmond Jabès's *Book of Questions*, translated by Rosmarie Waldrop? If not, I'll get it for you. I was rereading it today and it made me think of you.

Sarahlovely!

I haven't read Jabès!

How are *Oldest Boy*'s final weeks going? Is everyone excited? How does the puppet look, what's the puppet wearing these days?

I went to an amazing poetry reading last night: Timothy Donnelly read his poems: it was amazing, so funny and so full of heart and so brilliant. The way he writes—just as you're processing some deep image, you are provided with really nice, sensory, tactile, solid words and anaphoras and repetitions and rhymes that flash tiny pictures in your mind—then the deep and philosophical image that's been floating in your mind space clicks open and explodes, and only then does he move on to the next big deep one. It's really fine tuned for listening. I want to go to a reading of his with you.

The other element in the reading was John Donne poems set to kitschy punk rock, sung by a literary scholar from North London who REALLY REALLY wanted to be a rock musician. He was the backup vocals in Paul Muldoon's poet rock band. It was hilarious. He used a sound effect of BOINGOINGOING every time the flea was mentioned and . . . since he couldn't find any "bodice-ripping" samples, he used a zipper being quickly unzipped as a sound effect for the sexual-savaging images.

Thursday? Lunch? Brunch? Where to get a good pancake in this dump of a city?

XO
Max

P.S. I want to take a walk with you and hopefully see more skeleton puppets.

That winter, Max came to Brooklyn Heights for pancakes at the Iris Café. There was literary talk, and spiritual talk, as per usual.

I was working on my book of microessays, which I shared with Max; he was working at the literary magazine *Parnassus* and was full of stories about the people he was meeting. He even gave some of my poems to his friend, the extraordinary Elizabeth Metzger, who published one in the *Los Angeles Review of Books*. Yes, my first published poem was the result of my student, Max. We were becoming fellow writers—the teacher-student patina scrubbed away.

And things were looking up for Max. He got a teaching job at Columbia. He was in love. He had his twenty-third birthday, where he and Elizabeth sang karaoke to "A Whole New World." He was ebullient.

I also told Max about my recent adventure taking refuge in Tibetan Buddhism. I did the refuge ceremony with an English nun named Jetsunma Tenzin Palmo, who spent thirteen years in a cave in the Himalayas. I went to her teaching in New York. My readings about Tibetan Buddhism had changed me. There were few people with whom I would discuss my spiritual life—even the phrase "spiritual life" makes me feel a little queasy—but Max was so forthright about these matters, almost as though the life of the spirit had an objective life in the material world, and you could talk about the spirit with him as easily as you could talk about a table, or a piece of fruit.

At the end of our breakfast, Max stood up and declared he'd like to read a poem for me. I said: Out loud? In the café? Max nodded. Okay, I said. Max indicated that I should rise to receive the poem, which I did. And in a booming voice he read the poem out loud. I, a reticent Midwesterner, was deep inside my own mortification at listening to a poem aloud in public, even though I was grateful.

As we walked out of the café, on a cold day, scarfed and hatted, I must have mentioned that I was mortified. Max stopped in his tracks. "I embarrassed you?! Oh no!" He was undone. He was wild with apologetics, waving his arms. No, no, I tried to reassure him. I was happy to be embarrassed. It was just that my Midwestern soul could only bear so much attention in a small restaurant. I tried to clarify what I meant by embarrassment. Elizabeth Bishop once wrote to Robert Lowell about one of his poems: "I think one weeps over two kinds of embarrassment—& this is so embarrassing in the right way one wants to read it without really looking at it directly." If Max played the role of Lowell in his expansiveness, I often had the role of Bishop—looking for reduction, distillation, hoping to glimpse something sideways, indirectly.

But Max's charm involved being the most demonstrative, present-tense person in the room. After what he'd been through, he had no time for the Victorian slow reveal, for the poem that was almost-about-something, read in a quiet voice or put in a drawer. The directness of his gaze was such that you couldn't look away, and the sicker he got, the more direct his gaze was.

Perhaps it's worth mentioning that I come from a people (Midwestern, Catholic, Lutheran, Scandinavian, Irish—oh, and white) who are not traditionally demonstrative. Loving, absolutely. But demonstrations of love—more subtle. When my father was diagnosed with cancer when I was eighteen, we all had to learn to say *I love you* when we got off the phone. This felt odd at first—a muffled bird in the throat. But we got used to it. After my father died, my mother and sister and I continued to say the words to each other. But my family is Midwestern-tribal. No *I love you*'s to non-blood relatives.

Max was quite the opposite. If he loved you, he told you. Even if he'd only recently met you. Volubly, often, and sincerely.

Sarah!

I had such a nice lunch with you today. I'm so happy you took refuge with an awesome Himalaya-trekking white nun.

Here is the poem that mortified you today.

I will send you my essay on Buddhism and comedy as soon as I get high-resolution scans of the inserts completed.

WINTER POETRY

The color of death is purple
because death is more not less

Fainter? You thought?
No: the imperative of purple

Everything goes solid
blood and flesh purple and solid

Mirrors go purple when they die
I raised a mirror from when
she was a liquid baby

she scampered on her
little bathtub claw feet
right up into my heart

I bought her a glass yo-yo

when she was six
called her little treasure

She blossomed into a buxom mirror:
I braided her many sickle-shaped hairs
on the night of mirror prom
so she wouldn't look like a tacky disco ball

This is where the story gets factual:
She meets a beautiful boy at prom,
a spry frizzy pipe cleaner,
me from another dimension, set earlier in
the long salt of grief.

He "walked the dog."
Then they "went around the world."
Then they "slept."

He'll talk now—would you like to talk?
Hi.
We drank Chardonnay White Brand
a wine so dumb, you basically eat it.
I cleaned her pipes very slowly,
so she could breathe
in time to the Bee Gees' "Stayin' Alive."

She went purple.
I held her and held her
but it was Chance, holding her—
The Mistress With Ice Skate Blades for Teeth.

When the lake froze, we went skating.
Our hands were holding when it all went purple—
the lake, shivering with unreflective needles, the hands of leaving . . .

The Word Mystery fills the mouth with holes,
petite slices of tongue-loss.
It's the only purple word.

Death is not a purple word.
D is a purple letter. So are E & A & T & H.
But death is not a purple word. With death, something goes
    wrong:
somewhere we begin to share it, and cry,
and crying is *never* purple.

Max! I wasn't MORTIFIED! I meant the word "embarrassed" in the Elizabeth Bishop sense, in that I was moved that you read me your poem out loud.

Buddhism and comedy? Yes, please.

Did you like Mel Brooks as a child? I was obsessed.

xo,
Sarah

P.S. Here is my favorite poem by a second-grader, which I just unearthed from my desk from my days when I taught poetry to kids in the public schools:

> Try to sing
> while you think.
> A poem is
> not so hard
> if you sing
> and think.
> —Patrick, PS 17, Queens

And now Max's poetry was beginning to take off in the world. He gave a reading from *Aeons* at the 13th Street Repertory Theatre in New York, along with luminaries like Jean Valentine. At this time Max was full of brio, and hope. The tumors appeared to be stable. He had a book coming out and a wedding to plan.

Max's readings were extraordinary. Wearing a pink kimono, or a vintage canvas vest with nothing underneath, he would boom out his poems to packed houses, his voice reaching further than the back of the room. When there was an audience sitting onstage with him, he would rotate, wearing his pink kimono while declaiming poetry, arms outstretched, including everyone in his luminous pink gaze. At these moments, he was somehow like a rabbinical, Japanese Orpheus in drag. He was magnificent onstage.

Max had a hybrid nature; as a poet he reached into the solitary depths, but he also had an extroverted, flashy side that loved to perform, loved to dress up, and loved to hear theatrical gossip. He always loved hearing my show business stories, and he often had the insights of a world-weary, cigar-chewing producer. I'd tell him about an upcoming theatrical collaboration and he'd say, "I'd watch the shit out of that, Sarah!"

Here is a picture of him sitting next to Jean Valentine at his reading:

Dear Max,

I'm rereading your chapbook. It's an astonishment. What contemporary poet writes pentameter as gracefully as you:

> The opening and closing of my mouth
> is an attempt to fill my face with thought
> as kind and neat and unshaking as you.

So darn beautiful.

I hear in your work shades of mystics like Rumi and Julian of Norwich and Edmond Jabès; also the great love lyrics of the romantics; and also the plainspoken humor and irony that is none other than you.

Thanks for the gift of this book. I will treasure it.

I had the sensation reading it that we are just these containers with life and consciousness passing through us. I am home with the kids today (croup).

xoxo,
Sarah

Sarah:

This email made me smile enormously and made me feel all tingly warm. Thank you.

It meant the world to me to have you there at the reading. I felt your art-soul and teacher-soul and friend-soul sending me loving-kindness and listening closely to me.

I wrote several poems inspired by *The Oldest Boy* and I don't know if I ever showed any of them to you. Here's one I've been editing recently.

AFTER *THE OLDEST BOY*
For Brave Stan Possick

It is necessary to test you:
I place in front of you a legal pad,
a pretty blonde suede journal,
and a tape recorder.

Pick which is yours, I say.
Wordlessly, you take the legal pad, *his* old legal pad.

My excitement mounting, I place
a block of toffee, a box of Tic Tacs,
and an empty husk of Listerine PocketPak Breath Strips.

You reach for the Breath Strips, *his* Breath Strips.

There can be no doubt:
You are the reincarnation of my analyst.

Oh, Doc! How I've missed you these few years, teacher.
I missed your gray suit, and even thought of learning tennis.

Losing a teacher makes speech go out of tune;
I had to wrench out my tuning pegs
and plug them into the holes where my teeth fell out.

But you promised that you would reincarnate
into a Jewish body on the eastern seaboard

to preserve the dharma lineage, and be retaught our
knowledge.

Don't be scared, young man, I too was scared
to be identified as my analyst's old teacher.

Forever, we go back and forth like this,
we always have:
as others spend their reincarnations
first as mother and son, and then vice versa,
and then as prostitute and client,
then as child with string cheese and hungry bully—
our relationship is immutably locked.

We have an important thought that we share.
and thoughts are very important:

Consider a brain:
Neurons in patterns and chaos make a mind.

Consider a heaven:
Minds in patterns and chaos make a God.

What neurons are to thoughts, thoughts are to God.
God is real by virtue of being make-believe.

The connection between your mind and mine
is vital to God—

he protects it from death, reincarnating us again and again—
our love is God's thalamus.

(Here I am unloading this on a blinking six-year-old
with a lonely fish on his shirt.)

I'm sorry, but I *must* contradict you
again and again, as long as you live.
We must suffer together against your instincts.
We keep God from the fever.
If we fail, there will come a yellow flood,
and no kind boat of oak to save us.

Part Three:

New York and California, 2015–2016.
Or,
"I know you miss New York, but my neighbor just
dislocated his finger trying to kill a cockroach."

As Max worked furiously to finish writing another book of poetry and to graduate from Columbia, he was still in the thick of experimental trials and chemotherapy. He traveled quite a bit—to his doctor at the NIH in Washington, to his doctors and family in Los Angeles, and back to Sloan Kettering.

Sometimes I'd try to distract him during his long chemo sessions, or his vitamin C infusions, by texting him things like:

SARAH:
Who do you like better, Emily or Charlotte Brontë?

MAX:
Don't have a strong Brontë sister opinion.

SARAH:
Rilke or Rumi?

MAX:
Rumi.
Rilke is a bit of a fancy pants.
I mean I try to be like Rilke whether I like it or not.
But Rumi really had it going on.

SARAH:
Jane or Paul Bowles?
Mrs. Dalloway or Madame Bovary?
Wallace Shawn or Wallace Stevens?

MAX:

You're Sally, I'm Andre, let's have dinner, we can have soup.

SARAH:

Okay.

Why does a vitamin C infusion feel bad?

MAX:

Hyperacidifies the bloodstream. You get chills and insatiable thirst.

SARAH:

Sounds like Tantalus.

MAX:

Yeah, if he had to lug a boulder to the bathroom and back to the pond.

✳

But all the infusions and scans and treatments be damned; Max and Victoria were to get married that summer! Bizarrely and coincidentally, they were to be married at the very same restaurant where my husband and I had gotten married, in Topanga Canyon, almost a decade earlier. The restaurant is called Inn of the Seventh Ray; and it is appropriately romantic and more than little New Agey in terms of its bookstore selections. Max asked me to give a blessing at the wedding. Louise Glück was to be the minister.

Victoria and Max came over to our apartment to discuss the rituals for their wedding. Victoria being a scientist by training and not terribly interested in the world of the unseen, and Max being perhaps the most spiritually minded person I'd ever met (although irreligious), they had to figure out rituals that would suit both of them and their families. My husband being a doctor and scientist, they looked to us as a model of how to parse the world of the unseen and seen in ritual form.

Around this time Max and I decided to write letters more mindfully, hoping to make a little book out of them. I was hoping this project would distract Max from his illness. I also just plain liked getting his letters, and I wanted more of his writing out in the world. Our letters thus get longer.

I am okay, dear Sarah.

Cancer scans are last week of April. It's a big marker; I think it'll go okay or I'd feel shittier. The next trial I might end up on is called PD1. It blocks an enzyme that protects cancer cells, and allows the immune system to recognize and target cancer cells. It has been approved for melanoma and shows potential for Ewing's. It's such a strange world. The treatments I received at Yale are already on the verge of being obsolete. I'm living right at the time where if I hang on another few years, cancer might be a chronic illness like diabetes instead of a guaranteed terminal killer.

Victoria is doing well. She's stressed out by the wedding. This weekend I wanted to take her mind off of things so I planned a little trip with her. On Saturday I drove her to Doylestown, Pennsylvania, and we went to the Mercer Museum, an enormous poured-concrete cathedral crammed with everyday items from pre-Industrial Revolution America. When I say crammed, I mean it literally: the three-story central room has looms, apple-cider presses, whaling canoes, stagecoaches, and butter churners dangling from the ceiling and riveted onto every available inch of wall. Between tchotchke-encrusted arches are little alcoves devoted to tannery, sugar refining, glassmaking, stoves and cookware, etc., all cluttered with ephemera as if a messy artisan had just stepped out of a tiny well-equipped shop.

This dilettante anthropologist in the 1900s, Henry Mercer, was so obsessed with how life was changing after the Industrial Revolution that he bought up everything he could from about thirty or forty years before his time. Since nobody was particularly interested in seeing his thirty-year-old crap any more than we would be interested in seeing a museum of stuff from 1980, he decided to present the articles in a completely over-the-top fabulous, glutted fashion. He was literally defamiliarizing! He did a Shklovsky! And it worked. Could you imagine someone opening a museum full of immediately pre-internet paraphernalia? A cathedral with old Motorola flip phones and TI calculators for chandeliers and Moon Shoes forming a wreath over a vestibule devoted to Pre–Sedentary American Exercise crammed with spandex exercise pants, step-aerobics platforms, and light-up shoes?

There was a very dramatic moment at the museum. There is a scaffold for executions by hanging there. It's at the very top of the museum, in a large side room. Of course Victoria and I couldn't wait to see it. You walk over this ungainly wooden barrier, and there doesn't seem to be much in the room, except for a glass wall behind which there are some manacles and other prison-related bondage gear. Then, when you look back at the entrance and decide to leave and that they must've moved the scaffold, you see a sign fixed right by the door that says "Scaffold" and has an up arrow. You look up, and overhead there's a giant looming hangman's arm. The whole room is positioned underneath the scaffold, centered beneath the gaping-open drop-down floor where the condemned's feet go out from under him as he hangs. I noticed it first. Victoria said, "Where's the scaffold?" And I wordlessly pointed up and she put her hand on her heart. And I thought it was so interesting and spooky to put your hand on your heart as you suddenly imagine a noose tightening around your neck. And how interesting it is that the heart and the throat both need so much protection, and depend so much on one another to be needed by the body. And how the heartbeat and the breath are the two rhythms and the two vulnerabilities. And how scary, to look up, in a church, and see a hangman's arm. And how a church ceiling is really the top of an instrument of torture anyway, since churches are in the shapes of crosses.

I was going to tell you about the canoe trip we took the next day, and the olive oil bar full of old ladies that had plenty of free samples but they discouraged you from using their free-sample bread because it "interfered with the oil tasting" and how I nearly died of thirst quaffing down oil after oil with no fucking bread because I didn't want to seem gauche or disrespectful to their process—but I'm just going to leave it at those little bright glimmers, because I've gotten very carried away with this act of epistle.

Remind me to fill you in on my thoughts related to my thesis workshop. It's very late right now. And please tell me how you are! But be as brief (or verbose) as you want!

I love you,
Max

Dearest Max,

All day I've been thinking of your lovely letter and thinking what to write back, and thinking, let's write letters! Let's
write long letters once a week and one day make a little book
of them and sew them up with string.

I love your good report of the Mercer Museum. Clearly I
must visit.

I will anxiously await your April scans. And I'm heartened
that you feel well.

And I'm sorry that the wedding is stressful for the bride.
This is an archetype, she is merely behaving iconically for a
bride. I myself was a pregnant bride so I had hormonal ex-
cuses, but still, I was acting just as I should, sobbing into my
soup occasionally and browbeating the groom and screaming at my mother, who up until then I never had a cross word
with. If there is anything I can do to make the wedding less
stressful, let me know.

Other thoughts: I am reading Anne Carson's *Eros the
Bittersweet* and it is very brilliant. You should read it. I was
reading it on the subway. Next to me was a Hungarian woman
reading in Hungarian about tarot cards. On the other side was
a woman playing Scrabble on her phone. Across from me was

an African American woman reading a novel, *Orphan Train*. Next to her was a strange birdlike woman reading a tattered book aloud; I suppose she was praying, but it looked strange. And I thought—all these women and all these languages and all these books and here we are underground on a train.

Do you have Flannery O'Connor's prayer journal? It might be too Catholic for you but it's very beautiful so I might get it for you if you don't have it. I am also reading Wendy Wasserstein's biography and it makes me think about biographies and think that a high aspiration is to be biography-immune—to live a quiet and kind life and be like Atticus Finch whom no one would want to write a biography about because he said in public what he did in private so there were no big secrets to unearth.

Last night Hope pulled a chair out from under me when I was about to sit down and I fell down and hit my head and screamed: Goddamnit to hell, are you insane? And then she burst out crying and then I burst out crying. And I thought: How could I have said that to my daughter? Well, I did bang my head and I was surprised, but would Atticus Finch yell such a thing?

Those are my thoughts for the day. More long letters, I love them!

xxoox,
Sarah

ACT OF EPISTLE

Dearest Sarah,

Obviously we should do just that with our letters.

I think it's very touching that you thought "What would Atticus Finch do?" in the moment your maternity was put into crisis. Atticus is kind of a great mom. But you are too! I'm sure Hope seeing you cry was oddly helpful. It's nice to see other people cry when you cry—even if those people are the very ones who made you cry. And you were right: kids are insane. Is your tailbone okay?

You're also so right about trains! Trains are very significant. So much living energy and heat and heart in a place that we couldn't possibly survive in for more than a few hours is rather thrilling—we're like little fallen angels making a heaven out of hell. We managed to mash Hungarian and English interior monologues together in a little tube deep in the earth.

My friend John and I had a very significant train moment this weekend. On the train he was telling me about how, growing up as a devout Christian, he was always told that God was right there in front of him, and just slightly out of his reach. It would only take the slightest bit of faith and effort on his part to congress with God. And now, he feels like floating right in front of him at all times is the Good John. When he fails to be loving, or ambitious, or strong, it's made so much worse because he's so close to the Good John, a person he can tantalizingly channel for just a couple moments here or there. If he were just slightly less lazy, if he just reached slightly in front of him, he'd click into a perfect version of himself. And that perfect version keeps all the goodness of John, so John is no good at ALL except when he's the Good John.

That night, in the shower, feeling alienated, I imagined how different my interior life is from the interior life people imagine me having. How my mind disrupts my ability to listen and be empathic by wondering about what I look like at the moment, how the other person is receiving my nodding. How I can tune into the last few moments of someone's speaking and make a sensible reply even if the vast majority of my mental work as they spoke was the weaving a lurid tapestry of neurosis and vanity. I thought about if there is another Max, a Good Max, coating me like a shell. The two Maxes always share the same mouth and move our limbs the same way, since the outside world treats us the same way and makes us get hungry at the same time and summons our attention in unison. But Good Max might have all the right thoughts and feelings, and truly listen, and the good intentions (which I have) that make me behave well are fluent and pure and automatic in Good Max. And then I got very sad and jealous that there could be a Good Max living a happier life as a shell on top of me—protected from the wicked bad old heart in my core. But then I got happy—because I

realized all the people in the world who I cheat by not properly loving and attending to—they really WOULD get to
interact with a Good Max, who would shield them from having wasted their love and attention and energy on someone
as fearful, desirous, vengeful, delusive, as I am.

I was talking to Victoria about the Good Max shell and she
wondered if this is how psychiatrists feel—like they must
make a shell person on top of their core who won't be judg-
mental or allow their own personal biases to seep into a compassionate frame for the therapy. I said maybe therapists seek
perfection in Duality whereas Buddhism teaches us to seek
imperfection in Oneness. She said that out loud a few times
and really liked the way it felt to say it out loud. I explained
to her that this is what chiasmus feels like—and that chiasmus feels fucking awesome.

Speaking of: my thesis is getting fun: the working title is
Eight Reincarnations. There are eight sections. In each section there are four poems. Each section opens with one poem
from Heaven, continues into two from Earth, and closes with
one from the Underworld. The Heaven poems are all short
lyric addresses to women I love, the Earth poems are messier
poems with dialogue, Indian mythology, boudoir comedy,
family drama, and pasta, and the Underworld poems are ele-
gies. The Heaven poems are the only ones with dedications.

I had a crappy experience in thesis workshop where everyone favored poems that I found boring, and wanted to get rid

of poems that I find thrilling. But I've started editing the poems that thrill me, and I've just decided I need to get THEM to a point of unimpeachability and can ignore the ones other people like that I think are . . . um . . . they sort of wear muslin—you know what I mean?

I haven't been reading anything. Have I ever told you the Confucian proverb I like? "A few days without reading make conversation taste like food with no salt." I feel that way—sort of having lots of Unsalted Potato Chip conversations. I need one book to dig into—I was thinking about getting Julian of Norwich and going to town. I also have William James sitting around but someone I really respect intellectually hates him and I want to rest him so I can approach him without judgment. Or maybe I need to realize I don't want to read. Maybe I need to go on a hike.

About biography:

> Women bleed in private like animals.
> Men bleed in public like kings.*

Love,
Max

*A quote from a Sarah poem

Dear Good Max/Bad Max,

Sorry for the delay in writing. End of the semester combined with strep throat combined with throwing back out equals a long week. Whine whine, whinge whinge. At any rate, this morning Tony has taken the kids to violin and I am in bed, resting.

I was interested in your Manichaean view of your good outer shell and your vengeful bad inner core. It sort of reminds me of *Star Wars*, which we have been watching with the kids recently. Very Manichaean, with masks. I think you are very good, and too hard on Bad Max.

I finished a draft of my ethical slut play and read it in my living room this past week with actors. Maybe I'll send you an early draft. I would love to read some of your *Eight Reincarnations* poems, and I love the structure of the manuscript.

My thoughts are fogged in today, perhaps because of being horizontal. Unsalted potato chips!

And I'm sad for the earthquake in Nepal.

I will write more when my thoughts are more vertical. Consider this a placeholder . . .

At the end of April, the earthquake in Nepal killed nine thousand people.

And Max was about to have his own personal earthquake. His April scans showed more bad news. More tumor. His current regimen clearly wasn't working.

I met with Max after his bad news. He told me that he was afraid of death. I wanted Max to know that he could talk to me about his fear of death, that I wouldn't be squeamish, or deny the possibility. So I wrote Max the letter that follows, and the reply would come almost a year later.

Dearest Max,

A letter. And fair warning—this is a letter about the afterlife, so read on only if you wish to contemplate such things.

You told me yesterday that you are scared of death, that sometimes you leave the house and forget your wallet, and you think that death might be like that sensation: I left the house but forgot my body, my house, my New York City, my fiancée, my mother. The metaphor seemed apt. Walking out of the house, and forgetting, but not being sure quite what you've forgotten.

I think I may have told you once about a dream I had that comforted me about death. I'd had a biopsy of some breast tissue that looked questionable; it was normal, but I was dreaming and thinking of death. In my dream I was going to a Buddhist temple in India. The steps up were very high and gave me vertigo. When I got to the top I was going to make an offering, and I saw that monks were meditating and the odd thing was that they were able to meditate with their heads severed from the bodies, their heads lying peacefully on the ground next to their cross-legged bodies. I found this horrifying (the image of the severed heads) but also comforting. The monks could still meditate without their bodies. In other words, their consciousness persisted. After I saw these monks, I saw golden Buddhas racing, racing, all in gold. I was going to leave this tower and walk back down on steps all arranged like Legos, not glued in. As I walked down, the lapis Legos shifted under me and I faltered, falling. I was holding onto my daughter Anna's hand. When I reached the bottom, the stairway was gone, crumbled, and I apologized to a monk, and he said: *It's all right, they get arranged newly every day.*

I'm not sure why, but I found this dream to be a talisman that made me less afraid of death.

Once in my twenties I was in a car accident on Hope Street in Providence and we were blindsided and I hit my head and conked out and thought: This is how death comes, quickly. It was not frightening. Or even unsettling. It just was. It was dark at first. I saw a glimpse of how I would say goodbye to my body, and it seemed like quite a simple matter. Then I woke back up. Sometimes I think my whole life has been a dream since then.

Here is a question: if you had a choice, would you rather be orbited off into enlightenment after death, or would you rather be reborn a bodhisattva to come back and help others who are suffering? I know you are not a Buddhist per se, and you know me, I'm this strange syncretic wandering Catholic–former atheist–Thomas Merton admirer who just took refuge. I think you might already be a bodhisattva who has come back to help others. When I took a teaching from this wonderful Englishwoman, now a Tibetan nun, someone asked her a question about bodhisattvas, and she answered very plainly and antimetaphysically: "There are good people in this world. There are people who help. Look around you. There are many good people."

You, Max, are good. You don't know how many you've helped already.

The more I have looked into this reincarnation business the more I am convinced that we have had numberless lifetimes and will have numberless more. It does not necessarily make death less scary because we still lose everything we love, all this contingent matter, our identity in this lifetime, this person, this feeling of being situated, knowing, this web of love that we are cocooned in. But I do believe consciousness persists. I believe we get on a train, and the train is God knows what, the opposite of a train, going God knows where, but I do believe something travels and arrives somewhere. When I met you, you walked into my classroom, this wise luminous person, and I thought—it is not possible this young man is twenty. You had a wisdom that can only be accumulated from many lifetimes of suffering. Forgive my sermonizing. I am not a sermonizer by nature (I hope) but when you told me that you were afraid to die, I thought, Not many people like to discuss death, so I wanted to create an opening if you wanted to talk. I know I am not qualified.

The other dream that comforted me about death was about my father. I dreamed I saw him after he died, and in silver letters in the heavens was spelled out: *There is no God*. I turned to my father in the dream and asked: *But who wrote that in the heavens?* And he said: *Exactly*. At the time I was in Prague (of course) and reading *The Brothers Karamazov*, my father's favorite book. The dream seemed to be an answer to the questions the book was asking. That in the asking, the ability of consciousness to frame the phrase "There is no God," there was an answer, an ability of the thinker to contemplate God was enough proof of God's existence, or of an abiding, persisting consciousness.

I will pray to whatever god or God that your body gets better. And if your body doesn't get better in this lifetime, I will pray that we will meet up and recognize each other in the next lifetime, where probably you will be my teacher, as you once were previously.

Okay?

I am waiting for Anna to finish her violin lesson now. In the middle of writing this letter she emerged from her lesson and needed help blowing her nose. You can contemplate existence all you want, at the end of the day someone needs to blow their nose and hand you a dirty tissue.

I love you dear Max,
Sarah

P.S. I wrote you a small poem, attached.

AN AUTOMATED RECORDING FROM A HOSPITAL NEAR YOU

For Max

An X-ray of your soul shows
a general radiance

While the scan of your breath
shows only poetry

Waiting on the biopsy
of your imagination

but we suspect it cannot be contained.

Your body cannot contain you.
You're way too wide for that.

And if there is a Jewish heaven,
it is here, on earth,
on thirteenth street:
you, shouting poetry
in a crowded room,
circling,
and wearing a pink kimono.

Our letters at this point get stretched out over more silences—the silences probably include a great deal of chemotherapy on Max's end. And travel. And writing. And talking by phone, or in person.

Sometimes when Max wrote a new poem that he thought shared some inflection with me, he would say, "Sarah, you visited!" And then he would send me the poem. Like this:

Sarah!
You visited!

DIALOGUE OF THE TWO UNMERCIFULS

And surely you must be a merciful god—how glad I am to
meet you!

No, I am a just god. You will suffer forever.

But I believe in my heart you are merciful . . .

You do not believe in mercy in your heart.
You believe in the heavy tally of the day,
in the sharing of pork bones under the cloth,

in time taking itself with its love . . .

you listen to the bad imitations,
you eat Life cereal transmitted to your brain
by radio waves

Someone must, somewhere, believe in mercy. Surely this is
enough to save me.

You cannot have others believe in mercy for you.
You are not dice they blow on.

O God: will you look at my pain then?
It's not mercy, but I would like it.

To view the pain, one must be able to see
the whole animal, not only its face.

The long black mane cannot disappear
into the black neck's mantle:

a black fountain of hair must run
over the white air.

The animal will have run as far as it needs to
when his whole graph of hair is legible.

When you pull his hair,
you are pulling a map out of his neck.

Follow it to the X,
where he's the wild wet star
in the bathtub.

Dear Max,

So a long time ago I wrote a poem about your socks and
Evelyn Love who made them for you. Later, a composer
named Dan Messé asked me to collaborate on a song. I asked
if he could set the poem to music, which he did. Then when
you got your bad news I asked our mutual friend Bonnie if .
she would sing the song for you and Dan recorded it.

I thought I'd send it along for your listening pleasure.

Ms. Evelyn Love on Pond Street
She made me two green socks
Ms. Evelyn Love on Pond Street
with four daughters, pond and rocks

Ms. Evelyn Love on Pond Street
two blue socks she knit
for a boy, too thin, too loved, too bright,
too open, and too sick.

He's young and old,
and sometimes cold,
and when he cries as he does sometimes
he puts his blue socks on.

Ms. Evelyn Love on Pond Street
Two blue socks she knit
to give to me to give to him
to warm him when he walks

He's young and old,
and sometimes cold
and when he cries as he does sometimes
he puts his blue socks on.

Don't go, Max,
eat soup at home
Don't go, Max, write me a poem
Don't go, Max,
eat soup at home
Don't go, Max, write me a poem . . .

Sending you love on Mother's Day,
Sarah

Max wrote back in all caps:

SO BEYOND TOUCHED.

Dearest Max,

I am on a train to Providence and was thinking of you this morning vividly. How are you? I asked Elizabeth and she said you are getting stronger but still getting radiation every day.

Outside the windows are marshes. Inside the windows are commuters. How is a commuter like and unlike a marsh, I wonder. Inside the quiet car is its own culture of the sanctity of work. I asked to sit next to a woman whose purse was on her second seat and she seemed quite affronted and tersely allowed that I might sit there, but her sigh made me feel it would be a long ride, so I opted to sit next to a kind gentleman instead. The desire of people on the quiet car to protect their adjacent seats with purses reminds me of American privilege in general; it is an unspoken rule that the rich want an empty seat, a buffer, a space between them and the rest of the world, and if you violate this unspoken rule, you get an affronted sigh and an unpleasant ride.

It is the first quiet I feel like I've had in months so it seemed like a good time to write you a letter.

I think of you often and wonder how you are doing, body and mind. When should I visit? I will be in Providence for five days for rehearsals of *Melancholy Play* with music. Are we still doing that poetry reading together at 13th Street Rep? Let me know and I'll be there, most likely transported back to an earlier version of myself, terrified to read poetry out loud in public. Or maybe I've acquired some serenity in my old age.

At Penn Station today I stood in the spot where I stood around six months ago, *The Asian Journal of Thomas Merton* in my bag, after reading a section in the book in which Merton was being offered advice by a Tibetan lama to find a teacher. I thought, "I'm thirsty," and went to get a glass of water. Upon getting up, I saw a Tibetan lama in maroon robes named Lama Pema, who had advised me on *The Oldest Boy*. There he was standing quite naturally by a column in the midst of the dirty busy squalor of Penn Station, reading a book. I said, "Hello," and he said, "Hello," and he wasn't at all surprised to see me. "What are you reading?" I asked him. "An autobiography of His Holiness the Dalai Lama," he said, "that I've read a hundred times. What are you reading?" "Thomas Merton," I said, "about his travels to Asia." "Ah yes," he said and paged through my book. "Here is the handwriting of my teacher," he said, pointing to the page I was on. Merton had reproduced a handwritten letter from a Tibetan lama in his book. This did not seem extraordinary to the lama, but quite normal, that I should be reading the handwriting of his former teacher.

Then I bought water for both of us and we sat on the train together for two hours and he talked and held my gaze and said, laughing, "It is possible to smile. It is always possible." He entreated me to write a play on the life of the Buddha for children.

Are you able to read anything while you get your radiation? Are you able to read lighthearted things or are you reading big books right now? Should I send you a book?

I just read very quickly *American Wife*, which I found impossible to put down, but then again I read it because I am doing research on the Bush family for a play about whipping boys and political dynasties. I did two weeks of research and improvisation with a group of actors from NYU and it was fun and diverting and it was interesting to me to learn all about the "groom of the stool" who used to wipe the king's bottom and was in charge of all financial policies in England before the seventeenth century. This interested me, as Bush's nickname for Karl Rove was "turd blossom." I am looking for connections between the time of Charles I and II and of Bush one and two. I think there will be scenes of royal tennis.

Other than that I have been madly going to tap dance lessons and field trips with the children, and going to see plays for Tony voting purposes. The long wordless dance in *An American in Paris* was beautiful. A lot of things on Broadway are very tedious and cheerful.

Now I am going past a lot of water in Connecticut. Does Connecticut need to be this big? So many pools of water, so many empty seats.

I don't want to tax you with the task of writing, Max! But if you feel like it send me a little word.

Sending lots of love and can we find a time to meet in June before I go to Chicago?

xoxoxo,
Sarah

Sarah, Sarah, O My Sarah,

I was just going to call you today! And instead I woke up to this beautiful letter, and now, this evening, will write to you (and then, for good measure, I will call you tomorrow!).

How am I? It's been a brutal few weeks. My reaction to the gemcitabine and docetaxel chemotherapies was worse than anyone anticipated. (I feel betrayed more by gemcitabine, who has a beautiful name that filled me with hope. Docetaxel sounds like the name of a dog with red eyes and computer chips for teeth. Gemcitabine, on the other hand. Gem, Sight, and Beans: that sounds like the loveliest trinity, doesn't it? Pythagoras and India love lentils. Epicurus and India love gems. Greece and India both love Sight in their different ways. I really thought this chemical would understand my blood—that I was in good company.) My hair fell out and I ran out of platelets, so when my nose bled it bled for hours and I spat out dark tangerines of blood and had to go the hospital twice. My bones and joints felt screamingly pain-ful, so I swaddled myself in hot-water bottles. So no more Gemtax will ever Get Max. Right now I'm doing radiation therapy to my lymph nodes—fatigue is the only side effect. The radiation clinic is located in New Jersey so it's a very long commute. The next step shall be a more experimental drug, pembrolizumab, an anti-PD1 drug that helps the im-mune system recognize cancer as a foreign entity in the body.

There isn't a great deal of evidence for anti-PD1 in Ewing's, but it's something to try that will at least allow me to be myself and write and schmooze and go to lunch.

Commuters and marshes are both mostly water. You can't step in the same commuter or marsh twice. Both commuters and marshes make gurgling noises when they're upset. Marshes care less about what's in them than commuters, I think. I'm sorry that lady was so nasty. If she were a marsh and you were even something as detestable as a mosquito she would've welcomed you. I think you're brave for telling her to keep her empty seat and going to sit next to a more pleasant man. I often find myself paralyzed and obsequious once someone grudgingly allows me to sit next to them on a train. I think, "Oh, if I decide to sit somewhere else now, I'm snubbing their 'generosity' and singling them out and they'll feel guilty and then get angry at me for making them feel guilty." But in reality, they can either A) enjoy their privacy or B) grow from feeling guilty and C) I don't have to be around someone hostile.

We are the land of space, in America. I have a king-sized bed. I have white sheets on it so it looks even more fathomless. It's like sleeping on Moby-Dick. Ira Glass was talking about how migrant workers share their beds with people on other shifts. From a distance, it sounds kind of nice to imagine a bed being constantly occupied. That way the bed doesn't resent you for abandoning it all day, and keep you up that night as revenge. But I do like my big bed, and not having people rifle through my stuff—I'm ferociously protective of my privilege in that way. Where have you been in the world where people have healthier understandings of space? Isn't it weird that we own a lot of the stuff we make art about? Even space? Like we just own gardens and write poems about gardens we own? Or like Monet painted his garden?

Let's visit as soon as you're back from Providence. I will be going to Los Angeles for the next leg of treatment, starting right when you get to Chicago. Our show is still on if you're still willing! It's going to be explosively good. And you won't be nervous, because it will be the most hamish, supportive audience—as wide-eyed, cuddly, and socially awkward as tarsiers. I will send you a postcard of a jet-ski from Los Angeles if you find something equally obnoxious in Chicago to send me.

That handwriting story is unreal. It is possible to smile. I LOVE that—I think if I were to meditate in a frowny mood, that mantra could make a little void in my cheeks for the corner of my lips to fill. I haven't meditated in a long time. The only times I feel strong enough to, I just want to give myself over to something less challenging. What should I do about that? I feel guilty for talking so much about meditation and falling off from my practice. I'm glad you got Lama Pema a little globe of water. Do you think the reason for the meeting was so that you could hear "It is possible to smile"? I don't believe in reasons like that. It just seems so nice for it to happen—and if it happened to me I'd find a "reason" even if it wasn't one that I believed that the universe was involved in. What was his teacher's handwriting like?

I'm reading Lanny Hammer's biography of James Merrill. I just started yesterday and I haven't put it down. It is so so sparklingly written, and so so clearly a labor of deep love, and I'm finding it comforting to read about another person's childhood. There are mirrors in our backgrounds, some of which are very hard for me to deal with. Maybe I can learn a few things from his life—I've learned a lot from his poems. Merrill opened me up to being mystic. Before him I was All Atheist All Ancient Greece All Freud All the Time. JM got me into Haitian Voudon, Ouija, and his dippy Sandover mythology, and that was my first deep exposure to magic. I don't think I'd have the relationship with the Vedas, or with Buddhism, or with little magic bracelets and bits of cloth that I have were it not for good ole JM.

Was the Groom of the Stool GOOD at finance? Was he picked for finance or shit-scraping primarily? Turd Blossom—I can't. That's actually a really beautiful name. I've sometimes crapped very blossom-like turds. I will send a little prayer to Rove next time I flush a particular beauty down. I think a play about the Bushes and Charleses would be amazing and full of heart. I love GWB's paintings so so much. They're so full of heart and pathos and loneliness and humor.

When you said "Tony voting" I at first imagined Tony as in your husband Tony forcing you to see all plays and then vote on them to determine which ones to take him to. How is Tony voting? Are the shows free?

As this letter has gone all bloated already, I will limit myself to one other vocalization at you, which I've been meaning to ... er ... vocalize. It deals, of course, with soup. Radiation treatment has a very "just-for-you" feeling to it. They make a mold of your body that you lie in during every treatment, so you literally notch your ribcage into the machine. Two or three attendants lay sheets over you, and position your body lovingly every time. And the beam-gun is hooked up to this enormous garage door frame and hulking masses of metal whir around to get this little blue cylinder pointed exactly Goldilocks at your tumor. But the most heartbreakingly beautiful just-for-you thing is the sound the machine makes when the beam is emitted. Sarah, it sounds exactly like a tiny man with a tremor is opening up a can of soup inside the gun. There's an almost liquid echo once he opens the soup as the beam goes in. I swear I almost cried the first time I heard the little soup opening. It was the least likely place in the world to find soup, and to find someone tending to soup, and there it all was. Soup is the food that most allows your mouth to approximate silence—chewing is so very similar to speech. Soup's taste is also unlike the harsh, parsed specifics of language. If eating salad is like having to recite Gilbert and Sullivan's "Modern Major-General," then eating soup is like just having to hum the first few bars of "Good King Wenceslas." Nina Simone's song "Little Girl Blue" opens with a really graceful and sad rendition of "Good King

Wenceslas" and it feels holy. Holy as soup. I mention all this because I know your feelings about soup. When did you start feeling big things about soup? Where is soup in your plays these days? How hot do you like soup?

I love you, and now very much need to sleep. Call you in the morning.

Max

Dear almost heir to the Kentucky Fried Chicken fortune,

It was so good to hear your voice yesterday. And I'm so glad you are off the Gemtax and are onto the more soup-like radiation. I am glad they are tailor-making a radiation mold for your body, and that the attendants lovingly put the sheets over you. Sometimes I think Western medicine has so utterly lost this feeling of being tended to and touched, and those feelings of being tended to are so often the beginnings of feeling better. I remember when I first had acupuncture and the doctor himself laid a sheet over me and the needles, it made me feel like crying. Being tucked in, but by the doctor himself! I remember being sick as a child and my mother pulling a sheet over me, and, if I was hot, sometimes wafting the sheet gently up into the air first to create a bit of a breeze, and then it falling on my fevered body. I hope you are getting enough gentle sheet ministrations.

You ask me about soup. Why soup. I love what you say about the approximation of silence. Rather than the chewiness of language. For me I think there is something about the distillation process of making soup, and knowing that you are eating something distilled by time and patient human beings. Not chewing on an animal bone, but forgetting one's animal nature for the moment and sipping the distillation of flesh, not flesh itself, not even vegetable flesh. Not celery the thing, but the essence of celery after it's been boiled and the dross discarded. And of course soup comes in bowls, and I love bowls.

Then there's the fact that I fell in love with my husband at my twenty-sixth birthday party. I was having a soup party in Providence on Hope Street in our pink house. Sometimes I think the best meal would consist of three different soups, but you can't order that in a restaurant. So for my party I offered five different soups for dinner, to have my dream meal. There was roasted tomato soup, as I remember, and Tony made Indonesian peanut curry soup, the soup of love. Oh, it's such a good soup! I never enjoyed birthday parties before that twenty-sixth year because they always made me uncomfortable, the attention, accepting presents I might not like, and also the awfulness of big groups of people who I loved as individuals having to interact with each other. But at the soup party, I was so happy. And Tony put candles in my cake and carried the cake out to me, all lit up. And that was the night of our first kiss. And ever since then, I have enjoyed my birthday.

I decided that if I ran for office my slogan would be Consider Soup. Tony said that sounded very puritanical and I should change the slogan to Consider Sex. So one time for Valentine's Day I made him two different sets of sticky notes, one that said: Consider Soup. And one that said: Consider Sex. Perhaps Soup and Sex are the Apollo and Dionysus of the human spirit.

There is soup in my play *Late, A Cowboy Song* and I don't know if my other plays have soup.

It's a beautiful day in Providence and it's been nice to wander around this city. It's such a floating lopsided city, I adore it. My favorite bookstore, Cellar Stories, is still here, with the same smell of dust on books and the same fat proprietor who gave me a substantial discount on *The Anatomy of Melancholy*. I think in some funny way I became a writer wandering around this city—feeling the sweetness of solitude for the first time, walking around a new city by myself, and feeling slightly homeless.

What else . . . James Merrill! I don't know him as well as I should. I'm glad he gave you magic. I will read him. All atheist– all ancient Greece–all Freud all the time is tricky. I did that for a while too, mostly between the years thirteen and twenty-one. Well, not Freud. I never trusted Freud. Who was it who said Freud is good until you are facing your mortality and then you need Carl Jung? At a point I found Carl Jung and the *I Ching* (only use the Wilhelm translation) and then all bets were off.

I don't know if the Groom of the Stool was good at finance but I doubt it. It reminds me of this central problem in our democracy; we like to think we are in a meritocracy but often the person wiping the butt of the president, the man who happens to be close to power, is making decisions for all of us.

What else did you ask me? Tony voting. The shows are free. That makes them more enticing. I'd rather stay home and vote for my husband.

Off to rehearsal.

xoxox,
Sarah

We did in fact do a reading together at the 13th Street Repertory Theatre, pictured below. Max gave me the most personal introduction I have ever received. It went like this:

Sarah, you are wise. What does it mean to be wise? To make listening as much of a project as speaking. To make kindness heroic. To never ask of magic that it do anything other than heal. To never ask of excitement anything other than the present tense.

Some writing makes you feel like you've been all over the world. But Sarah, your writing makes me feel like I've been all over the world with you. I've been to Nepal with you: we've seen a puppet become an enlightened monk—which, in the very same moment of stage-magic, marks a mother losing her child. I've been on your couch while your daughter surprises you by want-ing not chocolate milk, but to open your heart's gate with a plastic key. We've been through the gates of the Underworld together and watched a father dance with a suitcase for lack of daughter.

These kinds of things can't happen without you, Sarah—the world just isn't like that until it's touched by you. I don't know which came into being to serve which—your imagination or your heart. Maybe your imagination came to serve your heart—to express your fathomless sensitivity—to safeguard me so I could learn all the real, hard things you have to teach me. Because

sometimes the real people in your real plays cry real
tears and suffer really, immensely, and sometimes finally.

Or maybe your imagination, all on its own, started pro-
ducing lovers' hair as leaking faucets, and cell phones
capable of transmitting conversation scraps to heaven—
and it made such overwhelmingly beautiful things that
it birthed your heart. Maybe your imagination was your
heart's own best or second-best mother, letting you live
hundreds of reincarnations in your mind, all during one
life span, and that made you who you are.

I often tell people to listen closely to what they're about
to hear—but I think everyone here will listen closely
to Sarah's reading no matter what. She's such a good
listener that she understands how to make her work a
joy to listen to.

When I was twenty and read my poems out loud in front of an audience I literally shook. Now I was in my early forties and it didn't feel too bad. I read a few poems by Max, a few of my short essays, and a few of my own poems. Max was forcing his teacher to come out of her poetic ostrich mode. And: Max was almost done with a full-length manuscript that would become *Four Reincarnations* and it was extraordinary.

Max at the poetry reading at 13th Street Repertory Theatre, introducing me.

Dear Max,

I'm rereading your manuscript, I love the first poem so much.
Your metaphysics are astonishing, and lucid.

Oh, I should go write a play now because I am in Rhode
Island and not parenting in Brooklyn. But sometimes I don't
feel ready to write a play. Maybe I'll read your book instead.
And have a walk.

I will look forward to reading your whole book. And when
you feel it's done I'll happily show it to some friends.

Another thing I love about your work is that I think you are
bringing us along where poetry needs to go, away from the
small and confessional into a big world, the world of death,
love, and metaphysics. You allow for the possibility of a
confessional mode in the details, but there is more additive
cosmology than saying, as so many post-Lowell poets do,
"What this all adds up to is *me*." It is like taking stock of the
nineteenth-century sublime, adding to it the death of God
and the Holocaust, taking stock of that reality, and going
forward with bravery, irony, the most compassionate sense
of humor, and of course your flights of language. I think
also your beautiful emphasis on dedications leads one away
from confessional solipsism into a personhood and personal
mode that is more about the other in the *I-Thou* Martin

Buber sense. So that lyric complicity is between self, dedica-
tee, reader, and world. In short, love. Not about the self with
the self, creating a series of mirrors and self-revelations. Oh,
dear Max. How lucky I am that I met you and you made me
love poetry again.

xoxo,
Sarah

Oh, Sarah! This leaves me inexpressibly happy. I feel understood very deeply, and by one of my all-time favorite writers
at that. It's just too much.

Also: officially, would you do us the honor of giving one of
the seven blessings at our wedding?

X

Dearest Max,

Oh! Of course! Would love to give you a blessing. Which one?? And how long?

Also, who is making soup for you?

Someone should be making soup for you.

xo,
Sarah

P.S. Also, I know you miss New York, but my neighbor just dislocated his finger trying to kill a cockroach.

Dearest Max,

I woke up this morning, opened up the poem of the day, hoped it was written by you, and when it wasn't, I pressed delete. I think of you often. How is everything going as the wedding approaches? Did you take a five-hour walk with Victoria on your anniversary? Are people still bothering you about cuff links? Are you going out every day and writing? I myself am not doing much writing since getting back to New York. I have decided I need to implement some rules for myself, like:

1) Never go into Manhattan for an errand.
2) Never have a meeting of any kind before noon.
3) Never agree to have a conference call, which will engender ten emails about when the conference call is, and then inevitably someone says, "Sorry, I can't do the conference call."

I keep fantasizing about writing a children's book, which would eliminate the need for conference calls about casting.

I am reading a book by Thupten Jinpa, who is the principal English translator for the Dalai Lama. He is quite extraordinary. I met him last year. His mom died giving birth to his younger sister in a labor camp in Nepal. His dad then became a monk, and he, at the age of seven, was left at an orphanage and became a monk. But he was always interested in languages, so he ended up getting his PhD at Cambridge and defrocked. He writes about various meditation practices, one of which is *tonglen*. Have you heard of tonglen? You breathe the suffering of others into your heart center, transform it, and send it back out. Or if you are suffering from an illness or anything else, you decide you are suffering on behalf of all the other people having the same kind of suffering, and you take their suffering into your heart and make it all into light beams and shoot it back out. It seems quite hard to do. And in a funny way, my being raised a Catholic, it smacks of playing Jesus, taking on the suffering of others. But apparently it's a very powerful technique to transform the mind and transform suffering.

I am busy trying to create an event that would do readings of *The Oldest Boy* in eight different cities on the anniversary of the earthquake in Nepal as a fund-raiser. I keep thinking more and more that one should not resist the notion that art can be helpful, was always meant to be helpful, in some fashion or other. And that Ezra Pound really fucked things up.

It is early morning and the kids are still sleeping and a flock of birds is wheeling happily outside my window. It looks like it will be another humid July day in New York, the kind of day where you feel you are being pressed into a crowded subway car even when you are not.

Have you been following the story of Atticus Finch's character being assassinated by his own author? Sort of interesting. I think I will not read the new Harper Lee book. But it raises interesting questions about authors, virtue, characters, and who owns them and their mythologies.

Well, I must make some breakfast and take the kids to weaving camp. Only in Brooklyn do young boys weave at summer camp. Well, and also sweatshops in other countries. William is very proud of his weaving, though. (They all are.) Oh, and I thought you would appreciate Anna's latest slogans that she's uttered: "My egg is a warrior." And: "Never insult a potato." The genesis of the first was an egg-tossing contest on the Fourth of July, in which Anna and I came in second place (she was very happy, first time she's placed in any competitive sport, and me too for that matter). The second was her defense of a limp wedding potato I was criticizing at my dear friend's wedding. (Wedding was magical, potato was limp.)

Write me a letter! Maybe you are in the Berkshires with Louise already! I am headed to Williamstown this weekend for a reading of *Dear Eli̧abeth*.

Lots of love,
Sarah

Dear Sarah,

Never insult a potato. He's probably just a scrambled poet.

I'm having a blast imagining you in an egg-tossing contest. I imagine your brow furrowing with furious focus as the competition drags on and other contenders fall by the wayside. And your eyes, your on-a-normal-day limitlessly deep and sensitive and completely steady eyes—eyes as steady as a bull's hoof in the ground—your eyes suddenly overlaid with a flashing, chaotic flame, and at its very center is a glowing egg yolk.

How does Anna recite her slogans? Does she chain them together as a macro-slogan? Or does she utter them at random as one-offs? I remember in sixth grade I had a "charging spell" that I thought, when uttered, would give me super-speed and act as an intimidation factor for my foes—who would all think I was very crazy. (And I was right about the second part, so maybe it really was magic.) I spent much of sixth-grade PE shouting "Zesty Pepperjack Sauce!" and throttling a Nerf soccer ball into people's torsos. I think I pulled the phrase from a Wendy's commercial. I would imitate the voice. It may've been my first exposure to a *Z* being exclaimed in a polemic/advertising setting. I remember being very captivated by the "hook" of the *Z*, so different from the dry recitative of *zoo* and *zebra* in alphabet books or

Scrabble games. I really love Anna's slogans, though. I think they're very wise. "My egg is a warrior" is very good feminism. I think Anna might be a political genius in the making—especially if the country is a fantastical country like Potatotanzania or maybe the United Soups of Ameregga.

The Nepal fundraiser sounds great! Would you like me to do a tiny grassroots reading in my home or in a little theater or someone else's basement with some loved ones? I can just round up as many people as I can (to read and to listen). You tell us what charity and we'll put a hat out for it! I think entertainment and art help the most by giving people pleasure instead of war. If we can take the money it makes and make it help people directly instead of putting it toward further pleasure, which, sadly, often entails obtaining raw materials via war, then we definitely should. It's funny and seems true for our world: you can't make art without first making war to get the materials you need.

I would personally find it very awkward if my dad left me to become a monk and then I became a monk. My daddy issues would definitely get in the way of my relationship with the divine. "Did DAD like this prayer when he first encountered it? Oh, DAD must've LOVED this part on nonattachment, must've made him feel just FINE about ABANDONING ME."

I like the sound of tonglen—your Jesus insight made me smile and laugh—you're totally right. It makes intuitive sense to me that it's easier to deal with your suffering as being the world's suffering—and it is much easier to fight for the world's well-being than for your own. I wrote a poem about how babies resting on your stomach make you a great meditator because minding your breath is a matter of being a good planet for them. It's for Dottie Lasky's baby, Hera. I'll attach it. Elizabeth Metzger says, "It's the first purely Maternal poem written by a Male poet in English." And that's mostly why I keep her around.

I'm growing quite tired and it's very late. ZESTY PEPPERJACK SAUCE! Alas, it just doesn't work like it used to—I feel no super-speed. I'll tell you about my day some other day—it was nice to twiddle around in yours for a while, so I'll just leave it at this.

I love you, Sarah,
Max

LOVE POEM FOR HERA
For H

I am Hera's planet,
and minding my breath
is a matter of giving her a good planet.

My outmost shell is her earth,
her sun and her water are mixed in my blood,
and curled in them is a diamond of air,
her sky, which I tug with my lungs.

How easy it is to mind my breath
when it determines
the rocking of her rubbery earth,
the warmth and wetness
of sun-rivers, the turbulence of the wind that serves
as all wind does
as a reminder to breathe—

Maybe Buddha wants us to think
of ourselves as the whole
universe so that when we breathe
we're supporting all the babies on
all the planets on
our chest—and that would make breathing
matter so much to us
that we could become
really great mediators.

Hera, tonight I drank your mother's milk.
I hoped my gut could show me your dreams:
The milk burned with iron—

how much brighter the stars in your dreams
than the moles on my body.

Dear Zesty Potato,

I love your childhood chant. I bet that was hugely disarm-
ing and distracting for your enemies. Sort of like Scottish
warriors painting their faces blue and not wearing any
underwear.

I am in Williamstown, just heard a reading of *Dear Elizabeth*
here.

I love your Hera poem. I also loved thinking of its real-life
context. I wondered whether it was worth a line describing
the reality of the context—a real baby named Hera on your
lap—so that we didn't assume it was all completely a metaphor about Hera the Greek goddess. But maybe you want
more of the epic than the confessional mode. I like the rub-
bing shoulders of the epic and the ordinary. That's my aesthetic prejudice.

Oh my God, I still have to finish writing your wedding
blessing!

Victoria and your family must be euphoric about your good
news after the new scans. Will you tell me more about them?
I just want to make sure I didn't dream it. No cancer in throat,
yes? That cancer walked away, banished, to the woods? As
in: gone? It is such wonderful news.

In answer to your question about Anna's slogans, they are one-offs and then I collect them. I like the United Soups of Ameregga. That might be a nice place to live. State soups instead of state flowers. Massachusetts would have clam chowder, Texas would have tortilla soup, who would get matzo ball soup? New York? California? Iowa could have corn chowder. Illinois could have Soup Secrets, the Lipton kind, out of a package. I could go on forever.

I like what you said about art and war. I want to write an essay about this topic and I may quote you. It's quiet in Williamstown with deer and bears and mountains. My friends from Vermont visited me here and told me all about their recent mushroom-foraging excursions. Maybe it is silly to live in a city?

Can't wait to see you very soon!

Lots of love,
Sarah

Everyone was relieved that Max would be well enough to dance at his own wedding, and not so immunocompromised that he couldn't be around big crowds. His scans showed that his treatment was working. The tumor in his throat was gone. He had an almost finished book. We were all euphoric.

✳

At his wedding, Max looked resplendent and very much in love. His head was clean-shaven, revealing his tattoo of the Hokusai crane.

Louise Glück presided over the ceremony, with many deadpan allusions to the difficulties of being married (she'd been married more than once). My husband and I danced under the tiny lights, astonished to be in the same place we'd been married nine years ago. At the end of the evening, I shared a dance with Max. I saw my husband out of the corner of my eye and brought him into the dance. We all three danced. Then Max's friends joined. Soon we were all dancing in an odd circular fashion, like some kind of ritual. And then my husband and I danced off into the night.

✳

I gave this blessing at the wedding. I later snuck it into a libretto for an opera of *Eurydice*, which pleased Max and Victoria:

MAX AND VICTORIA GET MARRIED: A BLESSING

Max and Victoria:
I wish you the blessing of imagination.

Every morning as you rise,
imagine that your beloved is perfect.

After a day with your wife, or your husband,
know that your beloved is imperfect.
But as you go to sleep,
imagine that your love is so big and so perfect
that it loves every small imperfection.

Imagine that you are a book,
and your beloved is a book.
How can a book read another book,
if a book can't read itself? Love.

Imagine that you are a book so patient and wise
that it learned to read itself,
so that it could read its favorite book.
Imagine this favorite book sleeps beside you every night
and reads you, while you sleep.

Imagine a love so patient, so kind,
that its poetic and scientific discoveries (which are boundless)
are dwarfed by the everyday ordinary imaginings
of why the beloved might be cranky,

what the beloved might desire for breakfast,
or the 108 ways the beloved is beautiful
when vexed, frightened, sad, sick, or hungry.

I wish you the splendor of quiet private imaginings
in one another's company
and the craggy arches of imagination
that connect you when you are far apart.

I also wish you two bowls of soup
that refill automatically.
And a fountain that refills every time you meet.

What is love, if not boundless imagination?
What is imagination, if not boundless love?
Victoria and Max: you are brave, you are kind, but most of
all you are loved.
May you experience the illimitable.
May your cup runneth over.

Dear Sarah,

Today we drove up to the Post Ranch Inn from Bacara. The drive was magnificent. I couldn't enjoy a large middle section of it, when the road veered from the coast, because I was sure I had taken the wrong highway. I wasn't worried about getting lost, but that I had ended up on an aesthetically inferior route, and that there was a better one that hugged the coast the whole way. If I couldn't enjoy it, I made sure Victoria couldn't either. Made her bury her head in maps and search for a nonexistent Atlantis highway that, even if found, would've been too far away for us to divert back to. The road came back to the coast and I calmed down.

The hotel is overwhelmingly beautiful. The beauty is quite eclipsing my ability to enjoy it. I feel a need to live up to it— to be peaceful and reflective. My yearning for peacefulness always has a secret agenda—what I really want, of course, is to cogitate sublimely and decorously in the aftershock of peace.

The room itself is all undulating panels of teak, healthy brown-and-beige rugs on caramel concrete, and 1970s Hotel Synthetic Cubism paintings with Mayan motifs. The lights are soft and reddish—everything is on a dimmer. The crown is the 180-degree balcony with an unobstructed view of the ocean. Its big honking diamond cross: the outdoor jacuzzi.

Kept precisely at 103 degrees, filtered by rocks, and totally unchlorinated—tastes like hot Evian.

The expense is palpable. And not just the monetary expense. Humans are expensive to nature, I'm realizing. Everywhere we go we replace nature with art. Our cities are so blighted with light and structure that the stars become invisible. As Victoria and I sat in the jacuzzi, I saw more stars than I have ever seen. Stars are really great—almost hallucinatory. It turns out that Victoria, as a child, had the same understanding of how the night sky worked as the ancient West Africans. (They came to it independently.) Both Victoria and the West Africans believed the night was a blanket and small holes poked in the blanket revealed a blistering cosmos of white light behind it. I'd much rather have the night sky for religious inspiration than the scrubby library of some Roman monk that smells like his bathroom. (And also *who* smells like his bathroom.) No wonder contemporary Christianity is so weird and fussy and bland. There are just too many people around the people who come up with its ideas.

One day I should try being peaceful without having a hidden agenda.

I love you,
Max

Dear Max,

I love your descriptions of the search for the *most* beautiful road, and also that particular hell for the writer—not wanting peace itself, but its aftershocks, so that one can write. If we could come to value peace itself, and not the contemplations it gave rise to, we might become enlightened there and then. But alas, for now, for this lifetime, we are attached to the fruits of peace—thoughts written down or thoughts rising.

I was reading Elaine Scarry's *On Beauty and Being Just*, some of which I love, some of which I think involves her creating a straw man and whacking away at it—but I love what she says about beauty always giving rise to the desire to replicate. Either in the mind—to write a sentence about it—or carnally—or taking a photograph. That there is this intrinsic desire to repeat beauty or reflect it.

I loved your wedding so much!

And I love the thought of you and Victoria staring at the stars, a dark blanket poked through with stars, protecting you while you sleep.

I meanwhile am at a swimming pool in San Diego trying to write my play about George and Jeb Bush. Tony and the kids and Tony's brother and sister have gone to the beach to see the seals, and I, crazy person that I am, stayed home to look up facts about Columba Bush.

Now try to enjoy some of your peace! What a smile Victoria has! Her face is all smile and eyes, luminous.

xo,
Sarah

Dear Sarah,

Victoria and I made a mandala today—which was the highlight of the trip thus far. I came up with much of the concept, helped mix the colors, and allowed Victoria to do almost all of the execution (which I find torturous and which she finds therapeutic). My artistic problem in general is twofold—one is that some of my ideas don't make sense and the other is that I have simply too many of them and they all bleed into muddy brown incoherence. With Victoria, I feel permission to make a million aesthetic demands—however implausible—because she is a little dazzled by me. But she only gets *enthusiastic* about the ideas that are coherent or manageable. The enthusiasm for the practical acts as a kind of sieve and solves both of my problems at once. We end up with JUST A FEW ideas and they are all WORKABLE. Our collaborative work, whether it's writing, drawing, whatever, has a very specific harmony to it as a result—if I'm willing to tackle mystery with promiscuity. She also brings to the table a fastidious, graceful respect to ornament that I lack. I attach a picture of the mandala. You will notice it's fountain themed and we wrote in pencil underneath it "How can a book read another book" and read it over and over again as we meditated and painted.

Max!

It is quite beautiful! Is it painted or out of sand? I am so moved my blessing made its way into your painting. You two are such wonderful complements, the execution and the inception—the first two hexagrams of the *I Ching*—the creative and the receptive, which makes the creative possible on earth. I feel like I should entitle this email "Epistle from the New Age." Well, actually, the *I Ching* is very ancient, not new at all. Speaking of New Age stuff, did Victoria tell you that I found out what "Inn of the Seventh Ray" is, in terms of the name? The seventh ray is a Vedic concept. Of course you got married at the site of a Vedic concept! I wonder why all of this ancient Eastern stuff got smacked with the title "New Age," as though Westerners just made it up in the seventies.

Also, did you slip a stone into my purse that says "teacher"? I found it this morning. I love it. You were probably busy getting married so it couldn't have been you. Maybe it was Amelia?

We went to SeaWorld yesterday (was that immoral of us?) and watched the dolphins leap and the whales splash, and I think my favorite was watching these peaceful aged turtles waft about above me in the light, eating the occasional bit of kelp. I think I'd like to swim with sea turtles one day.

Sending love!
Sarah

Dear Sarah,

Here's my baby.* Let's make it great. It's almost ready for the world, but it needs your compassion.

X

*By his "baby," Max meant the first draft of his poetry manuscript, which would become his extraordinary first full-length book of poetry, *Four Reincarnations*.

Dearest Max,

I peeked at the manuscript and the titles alone make me swoon with delight.

I had a dream last night and you were in it. And it made me want to know how you are doing. Also, I revised my ethical slut/ethical slaughter play (I'll attach it) if you want to read. I had a reading at Lincoln Center on Tuesday and it went well and it looks like they will do it next year.

How is your health? I read an article in the paper about a playwright I know named Christopher Shinn. What I didn't know is that he had your same cancer and recovered completely. That seemed like a good omen.

xoxo,
Sarah

Dear Sarah,

Tell me what you think.

HOSPICE

My head is a bed on fire.

You leave the bed
and leave me without thought.

The springs want to embrace each other,
but they're afraid if they break

their spiral, they will never
be able to hold anyone.

I wish you would let me know
how difficult it is to love me.

Then I would know you love me
beneath all that difficulty.

You are tending not only to me,
you tell me, but to your other child—air,

and air puts his feet in my slippers,
and air scrubs his teeth on my brush,

and wherever my demands are not—
there are his!

And we must learn to share a bed,
we must learn to share a body,

the money is running low:
we will have to split one needle

this winter—one end for me,
one end for air.

Dear Max:

BEAUTIFUL.

Sarah dear,

What a joy to read "Slutplay." Or, rather, travel through its many portals. I have gotten so caught up in studying you that it's started to feel like you're writing to me personally.

Pythagoras, the line between a goat and a dog, the fire of love that cleanses without sanitizing, for you cannot *eat* something slathered in soap—the fire that makes murder and meal of the same meat—

How are you the pendulum-weight holding down so many of my cosmic ropes?

I love George very much—and I have been trying to put into words for a while what she says when she says, "Our objective in the West is to make ourselves irreplaceable . . . and then we die."

I do have one reaction to share that was very personal, and I hope you don't mind. I was really upset with Pip's rationale for choosing to eat meat. I, of course, think she needs to eat meat or there's no play! And it makes sense for her to come from being vegetarian.

But the justification she uses ("I needed protein—I was sick") put a pit in my stomach. I have recurring nightmares of doctors, or my mother, pressuring me to eat meat if my cancer progresses. I have a nightmare where my family cuts me off because they're convinced that if I were to eat more protein, I'd live—and that my vegetarianism is killing me.

What makes this especially difficult is that there is a gross distortion of the importance of protein in Western culture —primarily rooted in large amounts of money poured into the for-profit nutritional industry by meat and milk lobbies. There is large-scale epidemiological as well as rigorous bio-logical evidence that indicates we need much less protein than is commonly accepted. More than that—there are many plant-based alternatives that are just as protein- and iron-rich as meat counterparts. Beans and brown rice alone pro-vide all the amino acid chains found in animal proteins. (I'm starting to feel weird and preachy, so I'm going to go back to my feelings and away from Facts.)

I have a vegetarian friend who grew up vegetarian, and his schoolmates' parents would harass him and claim he was go-ing to be sickly and stunted and malnourished because of his diet. They even tried to sneak meat into him. All because of "the need for protein."

I'm terrified that were I to watch "Slutplay" with my mom, or with one of my skeptical friends, they'd turn to me and say, "Max—you need to be like Pip—see?! Even the most animal-conscious people have to eat animals for the protein when their health demands it."

Other than that, I love every bloody feather. The fact that the eggs die was so moving. If women identify food-pleasure with nurturing something to life, and men with slaughtering something to death, then who knew EGGS—brought and nurtured into life and then neglected and slaughtered to death—could be so *ANDROGYNOUS*!

I also found the reveal that the sevensome was a foursome extremely touching. It took Ecstasy and put it where it belongs—in Intimacy. The truly loved-and-loving nucleus of people—of course they are the only ones capable of transcending their bodies together, not with strangers and strange rites.

Could the bird appear once more, somewhere? I want a third moment with the bird.

On my end—I'm flying back to Los Angeles for more PD1. I'll be back in New York on Tuesday. I'm pretty exhausted by all the back-and-forth travel, but more than anything else it's the damned Zolinza dragging my feet around.

The Columbia job is mildly sad, and mildly rewarding. The freshmen are so frustrated—they've always been the best at everything and now they're not. And Columbia's pedagogy is to Allow the Writer to Retain Ownership of Their Piece at All Times, which means a lot of leading Socratic questioning instead of just saying, "Yo—change that preposition and try moving this paragraph to the top."

My best teachers have made me feel like my piece of writing was alive, like it had value distinct from Me and my Perceived Ownership. Enough time spent with a good teacher and eventually there is a new little me in my head willing to take my piece away from me.

I haven't written anything new in a while, and it's upsetting. I think *Eight Reincarnations* isn't right as a title anymore. Jabès is in my head a lot. I've put a question in front of each of the four sections. (What is love? Do you love me? Will you marry me? Where have you gone?) I wanted to call the book *Four Questions* but I'm worried it's too Passover. Maybe *Four Questions On Love*. Or *Four Reincarnations*.

It looks better with the new poem in the beginning—and I changed the first line to "The bed is on fire, and are you laughing?" which is a riff on the *Dharma Padda* ("The world is on fire, and are you laughing?"). The pasta poems are gone—except the one postscript.

I wish I could call the book *Four Women* (Melissa, Charlotte, Victoria, Mom), like the Nina Simone song, but it just won't get across anything.

I'm trying to write a series of memories on coffee for *Berfrois*. They interview poets on coffee. I don't drink coffee. But my mom drinking coffee was maybe my first experience with chemical magic—she just became a different person after swallowing the potion. Her skin would glow, she would smile.

And I think I expected antidepressants and chemo and everything would work like that—just like coffee—magic and instant and you don't even think about it. So I might talk about that as a potential source of mixed expectations in my life.

Victoria and I took a couple to Risotteria Melotti on a double date. I got the red wine risotto, which came in a cheese cup and tasted distinctly like sloppy joe. Next time: mushroom. The hostess remembered me!

Chris Shinn is a friend of mine and we've been treated at the NIH together! The trial that was successful for him was the same one that failed me. I haven't read the article—I can't quite bring myself to. . . . These trials buy us a year or two, and then something else pops up. Of course, I'm rooting with my very roots—but in reality, since there's no long-term study done on this trial, there's really no way of knowing how long it works. If we look at the history of "successful trials" in Ewing's (insulin-like growth factor, PARP inhibition)—they work a bit and then they don't.

What happened in your dream?

Give me an update.

I really do love you a lot.

Dear Max,

Thanks so much for all your wonderful thoughts about the play. I'm interested in your reaction about the iron and protein. Pip is a wild creature but also slightly based on a person I know who used to be a vegetarian and wanted more iron so slaughters her own animals and eats them.

I have really no medical opinion about this—I'm only interested in the character. But I suppose in a play that looks at the politics of eating animals somewhat, I should look a little more closely at the ramifications. I hardly eat meat either and am often told by Chinese medicine people that I need to eat more animals. But I've read the China study and it seems that eating meat and dairy is very bad for your health. I don't think you need to eat meat to get your iron up! Perhaps one of the other characters in the play could express this thought. Someone like Freddie, who continues to be a vegetarian. I guess the lucky thing about plays is that they are multivocal so can contain a wide array of opinions on one subject.

I like the title *Four Questions about Love*.

I also like the title *Eight Reincarnations*.

I like the idea of structuring each section with questions.

I also like the title *Four Women* but I do think that implies the book will be a Neruda-like lovefest and I think the book has broader concerns. ("How can one have broader concerns than love?" you might ask.) Well, I think you're also looking at death, the body, selfhood, and God. Which is all love anyway. But still. It feels bigger than those four women. I also don't like *Four Women* because it gives the four women equal weight somehow and Victoria is The Woman rather than one in four. Those are my two cents.

Is

Four Questions about Love and Four Reincarnations

a bad title?

I always want to have my cake and eat it too. It's a problem. Okay, I will write more soon. I have to call my sister back.

xoxo,
Sarah

I like the idea of Freddie voicing my idea!

I am going with *Four Reincarnations* for right now, but I also liked the idea *Four Oracles*—and I ask a question of a different Oracle at the beginning of each part.

Working on a poem where I'm a little 100-percent sign that slowly dissolves into lower percentages in my mother's hand, and decimal points pop up as tumors, and then the decimals turn me into binary code which runs a machine which prints out receipts that my mother has to sign with her sadness to produce proof of receipt of child.

Tomorrow is PD1 treatment. Inhale.

Exhale,
Max

GIVING HER 100%

For my best friend, my protector, my mom

There is a world where
all of a son's battles
are fought by his mother
and in this world
I am one of the great Heroes.

In immaculate black boots
and a war-girdle of linen
she stakes herself in the front lines.

She wields a sorcery stick that calls
bladed chariots, supply caravans, and tornadoes
from over the horizon,
and she's had just about enough of your nonsense.

Don't give her that lip.
My mother only accepts commands
from battle itself—
and her allies, dazzled by the purity,
the sincerity, the adoration
with which she gazes into Danger's eyes,
accept her hand to kiss.

And remember: before you try to tell her
that she's overvaluing me,
wasting her time on this enterprise,

and wouldn't she be better off
cutting her losses, finding a new, healthier champion?
My mother signs my name
in the blood of my enemies
and refers to this as her only contract.

Unfortunately, in another world,
mothers don't fight the battles
of their sons,
they have their cancers.

In this world, Mother does not fight,
but counts alone.

I see you over there,
dark bead threaded on a string of fire,

I see you, running a black abacus
as water drips on your head
from the ceiling on a dry day,
a large pool forming at your feet.

When you held me up
from the waters—
a flexing, thrashing 100%,
glowing white in your palms—

how strong I must've looked
as the waters receded,

like I could've lived just as easy
on air, or water, or blood (and in fact,
had lived on all three of yours).

And how sad to have watched
97%,

73%, and then
the blinking and flashing,

that unhealthy spot near my tail—
the decimal—44.2%,

and more decimals making me code
that runs a program for a receipt-generating machine,

and an infinite ribbon of paper
making you scribble out your sadness
to confirm your receipt of child

and in the blinking, colorless increase,
impossible to attend to
a crying boy
you put in a basket of reeds

to secure him through this
white river's growth:

I will weather this storm—I promise
I can feel you up there counting,

and I know that if I am too weak—
you'll prop me up on your hands
like when I was a baby,
and you'll let me count,
but I'll be counting on you.

That week, I opened my play *Dear Elizabeth* in New York. I offered Max tickets but he wrote that he was in Cancerland, California, and therefore unable to come.

Then I got a voice mail from Max telling me he had bad news. There were blips on his scan, blips that he'd hoped were innocuous. But the biopsies showed them to be not innocuous. There were new tumors in his lungs and throat, and he was going into emergency surgery in Los Angeles to get them taken out. He said that a little robot would march into his lungs and try to get out the tumor.

He sent a note to all of his friends on October 29, to update us, saying:

> If you need to reach me, or send me anything I'll hopefully have access to email, but who knows how alert I'll be. You can grab Victoria if you need something and I'm not responding. Please don't ask her too many questions about what the logistics look like, or where and when I'll be where and when—we just don't know that right now.
>
> FOR INSTANCE:
>
> Good message: "Wish Max well! No need to reply!"
>
> Bad message: "When is Max next going to the bathroom, and in what city is it in—I'd like to bring my schnauzer to visit him; he's a good luck healing massage schnauzer from Ireland. Is Max going to die? How often will Max die? Can he attend my event in four months?"

*

I was always impressed by Max's sense of humor in his group emails. He knew we were all hungry to hear from him, and he tamed us with his humor.

I talked to Max on the phone after his surgery. He had a new, worrisome cough. It sounded like a seal bark. We talked about life, death, and, as usual, what we were reading. I suggested Maggie Nelson and Montaigne. Max was scared, and I was worried. But he still made me laugh. And I tried not to make him laugh in return, because it elicited the seal-bark cough.

I wrote Max a poem for his robot surgery.

When I see you I am happy
even when you're sad.
Meet me at the carousel
in this life or the next.
Meet me at the carousel
I'll be wearing red.

You said girls named Sarah
generally have nice hair-a.
You say I am a marble steadying
your swimming hammock.
Max, swing gentle.

Robot, march into your lungs today
and cut out all the little death.
You want more drafts,
more delusions.
And I want more talk with you,
more word collusion.

Meet me at the carousel
in this life or the next.
I will be carrying a draft of a poem
and a bowl of soup.
You will be carrying a pencil and a spoon.
There is time. There is soon.
There is a yellow hospital moon.

✳

That January, the poet C. D. Wright died. I'd known her when I was a playwriting student at Brown. I loved her poems, and though I didn't know her well, I adored her person. There was also more bad news from Max about his treatments. He would need surgery to fuse a lung to a chest wall so blood didn't come pouring into his lungs. Before his wedding, it seemed possible that a miracle cure was on a distant horizon, ever receding, always just a month away. Now, only five months later, it felt like his doctors were in triage mode. I sent Max a short poem:

> There is no lyricism for this,
> the insurrection of your body
> this particular week.
>
> This week, C. D. Wright's body
> left her while sleeping.
> Then her poetry walked off the bed
> straight into the long dark hall.
>
> Or did she leave the lights on
> before she went to sleep.

Sarah:

This is the best poem.

I'm also very sorry about the loss of your friend.

I haven't had you visit in a while, and even though I've loved my writing recently, I really really love it deep in my heart when you visit.

I love you,
Max

Max attached a poem to that letter:

YOUR NEXT DATE ALONE
For Victoria

The stage is empty.
How do we fill it?
With music.

The words will be the play,
and the tune will be the body
carrying the words,
shaking with tears

the towel torn
so what he'd like hidden
is exposed—

where his flesh is like a bruised heart.

Music is the wisdom
of words in a body:

if you wish to see me
you'll have to sing.

I will soon have none
of the ways earth plays
along with the soul:
no grass, no wind.

Dearest Max,

This poem is exquisitely beautiful. I love it. It's Orphean. And something Neruda. And something entirely you.

I've been thinking of you so much this week and haven't wanted to pester you.

Elizabeth tells me they have been draining your lungs and it's agony, and that you are to have surgery to fuse a wall inside your chest so the blood doesn't come pouring into your lungs. Is that about right? Oh, Max.

I dreamed the other night we were all at your family's house. You were worried about getting your manuscript into print. You were poring over it. I dreamed another night that you were saying goodbye to the people you love and I woke up weeping.

I wish I could put some wisdom into these little words or some comfort and send it through the ether. I'd rather sit with you and hold your hand and make you soup.

As it is, I am wrapped in a towel after cleaning up the vomit of the twins (there is a virus going around the outer boroughs at lightning speed) and the twins are wandering around in bathrobes, vomiting into buckets and holding Popsicles and watching *Scooby-Doo*.

I have a little present to send you—a blue medicine Buddha that Anna and I picked out for you.

What could I tell you that would amuse you? Maybe I will attach my *New York Times Book Review* By the Book interview, where I mention you as one of my favorite contemporary writers.

Send me a little word here or there when you are able.

Lots of love,
Sarah

Dear Sarah,

I loved reading your By the Book. Especially the "women who get raped a lot. But in a literary way." I also think that's the best list I've been included on.

I'll call you today and if you can talk we'll catch up. It's been by far the most trying time of my life. I am myself for maybe an hour or two a day, and the rest of the time is anger or despair or overwhelming bodily discomfort. Los Angeles is hard. I feel like one of those loathed literary ladies from your interview. Everyone around me is a Hemingway bull and I'm a china shop.

I think that the best thing I can do at this point is accept the state of affairs—that the equanimity in my life right now will have to be more radical than the kind that attempts to re-balance the heart and the body so they suffer less. My equanimity just has to be forbearance and forgiveness every two or three seconds for the condition I find myself in. Maybe, at the end, there is only the First Noble Truth—all four fold back into the First. Or perhaps it's enough for me, right now, to just be dealing with this: there is suffering.

Thank you for dreaming about me. I'm happy I made you cry. It means you love me and my situation is suitably dramatic. But I'm sad I made you cry because I love you and don't want you to cry.

Are the kids vomiting and then just diving back on the Popsicles? Is that safe? It's hilarious, at least. I hated *Scooby-Doo* when I was a kid—ESPECIALLY while sick. It's a show so banal that its banality is transparent even to children, and I think some of my first feelings of cynicism were a bad mood from a flu combined with an eye-rolling certainty that the monster on *Scooby-Doo* was a man in a mask trying to profit, despite the stilted, idiotic, highly mannered air with which the Mystery Gang treated the case. It was like Noh theater and kitsch, and at the time neither made sense, and I still hate the latter.

Send over Buddha MD stat. He can't be any harder on my stomach than the alisertib. And I could use God in my life, but a tiny God whom I can chat with and who has physical eyes to watch me groan and will maybe start to care enough to intervene as a result. It's weird that we expect compassion from gods that aren't idols—don't we see how much laying eyes on suffering and the touch of someone's hand on our body motivates us to save others? Also strange that Buddhism, with an emphasis on nonidentity and the elevation of consciousness to an impersonal all-encompassing empathy, still gets that we need idols. And that Christendom, with its private egotistical relationships with God where you pray for what you want, and Judaism, with its numberless sacrificial rites to get exactly what you want out of God, became the world's idol-smashers. (Not surprising that the Russian mystics understood why idols were important and brought them back.) Maybe Buddhism just understands that WE are the ones with limitations, who need little blue Buddha MDs, and can be met where we're at. And it took a real nutso like Moses to imagine God threatened by something that isn't Him, but helps us feel Him in our hearts. Moses probably felt threatened when his wife masturbated—it's the same thing, really.

Maybe you should come out here and make soup soon. I don't know if I'll make it back to New York. We'll discuss on the phone.

Love you,
Max

Dearest Max,

I love this letter, and reading it, I can see clearly that you are yourself for at least part of the day, while you are writing letters. That is a small blessing.

You made me laugh about *Scooby-Doo*. Clearly you were an elevated child. Mine are happily slack-jawed in front of *Scooby-Doo* for hours at a time when they have stomach bugs, which is good for me, at least, as I run around with bleach spray and rice crackers, waiting for the next explosion.

I so love your reverie about idols in different religions. And Moses's wife. Yes, why be threatened by idols, I wonder . . . it's a very interesting question. The blue Buddha will be on his way tomorrow. The UPS store today closed at 5:00 p.m.; I got there at 5:01 with a dry-heaving child in tow.

About me and crying—it made me laugh what you said about being suitably dramatic. But here is one serious thing—I have an aspiration to be one person in your life whom you do not have to comfort through your illness. So don't worry if I ever cry in a dream or otherwise. The main thing is you. And you finding your equanimity, however hard fucking won.

About me and soup. Yes, let's discuss. I wonder how/when I could come out. I am flying to Louisville for first rehearsals of the Peter Pan play in February for a week (I should send you the video of me flying in my flying harness). Maybe there would be a way for me to tack an Los Angeles part of the trip onto one of the Louisville trips. In any case, call anytime. I am here.

Oh, and on C. D. Wright—what a shock. She and I weren't close at Brown but we were friendly, and she was always the most approachable poet in the poetry department. She had such a warm wonderful twang and I love her poetry. My playwright friend recalled her once saying at a cocktail party: "I'd rather fuck a dog than go to the theater." That might have been apocryphal. I did adore her from afar though. She was truly generous and luminous. Maybe God wanted to read more poetry this week. He'd had enough of prose.

I'm putting the kids to bed now but around all evening and all of tomorrow if you want to talk. I don't want to bother you while you're resting, let me know a good time of day to pester you. And sending love to your good mom and Victoria, too.

Lots of love,
Sarah

Part Four:
_____

California, 2016.

Or,

"Heavens are all alike, the people who make them are all artists."

At this point Max moved into his mother's house in California full time. It was no good, his shuttling back and forth to New York to teach and to see friends. He needed care. He needed family. He needed to be near the hospital.

I had sent Max a letter almost a year earlier about the afterlife, following a conversation in which he told me he was afraid to die. Max hadn't answered the letter then; it was too much. But now, out of the blue, he answered.

Sarah,

It's taken me just over a year to attempt to reply to this letter. I've told you often how much it means to me, and how I intend to reply—but it's difficult to try and communicate back to something that loves you so much it burns you. I have a natural tendency to cut people off mid-sentence—to barely hear what they say before trying to touch it with my own mouth. I think my silence over this letter tells you how deep it goes. Thank you. This letter is silver, in the sky. And in the end, that's probably all that will matter.

But also, I've been afraid to respond in part because you are deep in me. You are beneath belief—you are voice itself. When I write, I often feel the language coming out to be yours. (Of course, the language is demented and dizzied by the hedge maze that stands between my inspiration and the page. And it's a great hedge maze. It's proprietary. The hedges are actually impossibly large onion plants.)

You, in fact, are me. Yet above voice, there is belief—perhaps situated on a pile of priceless blue Legos—and I find myself unable to believe in a committed way in the afterlife that you have torn from your dreams, your near deaths, your tears, and your inspiration, and have given to me as a glowing gift. It's weird. Your letter feels like a bone that has grown out of my body, around which I am unable to form flesh. It's terrifying.

The problem is with consciousness persisting, and what is meant by that.

For me, consciousness emerges bit by bit. An ant is a bit conscious. A dog, a bit more. Really all that's needed for consciousness is for information to be stored and then exercised. The system of information, if it gets complicated enough, will eventually become self-referential, and at that point it's thinking. I'm a Turing boy, in my heart, and a Hume boy.

I think a trillion planets in different galaxies, moving with a degree of regularity and interrelatedness, could have a mind. I think the act of speaking, in which information travels from brain to brain, if it is spread among enough brains, could form its own consciousness. This last idea I came to after I saw *The Oldest Boy* and wept and wept, thinking that the monk and Tenzin, sharing the same set of ideas in the same language over and over again, could be a crucially stable line of code in the conversation that is God. I wrote a poem for you about this, where my shrink and I are like Tenzin and the monk.

But the limitless potential for consciousness means another thing: it's really sloppy. The consciousness in our brain is not a coherent force, not something perfected and organized, but a phenomenon of trapping in as much of the world as we can as it comes to us through a welter of chaotic channels. Because our brain is made up of many tiny scraps of code, many little machines, many little ants, and is not one perfectly engineered program. As human beings evolved, we picked up useful little things for our brain to do, and over time they crashed together into what we are.

We actually have, in our brain, two different visual processing systems—one that provides us with color and light and shape and the world as we know it, and another one that evolved much earlier, when we were shrews, that can only tell whether something is horizontal or vertical, and whether it is approaching from the left or right side of us. This shrew brain isn't normally active in a human, but when people are blinded by strokes, they can, with close to 100 percent accuracy, take a cartridge and stick it in a slot that's either vertical or horizontal and positioned to their left or right. It seems miraculous to the blind people—they say they aren't seeing anything, but can feel jaggedness through their eyes.

The brain is full of first and second drafts of ways of thinking. The parts of the brain that are in use exist for their own sake, and on their own terms. And sometimes they conflict with one another. Sometimes we just outright ignore parts of our consciousness. Every time you aren't tuning into the sound of a clock ticking in your room, it's not because you aren't hearing it. The part of your brain hearing it is just being damped and muted by other parts. Consciousness is almost an ecosystem of sensations, with predators, prey, weather patterns, and natural resources. Consciousness as a sensation, as a system, all comes together kind of by accident, and we make sense of it all because we have to.

So with that in mind, what can I say about consciousness persisting? Broken down, the storm of codes that happen to coexist in my brain seem to me perfectly willing to part from one another. Preserving them would be a much more difficult task for God than if my consciousness were a whole Thing. My Soul isn't a fish, it's an Ocean with waves breaking in a particular moment in time. And that's another thing: I think I am time. But not Time. Rather, I am my time.

And funnily enough, Buddhism has gotten me to feel this way more than anything else. Since you last wrote, as you know, I've started meditating and reading Buddhist texts. Meditation has been stripping me back, and when you strip me back, you find paradox. When Buddha talks about Being and Not Being, Cause and Effect being both something to liberate yourself from and something that's essential—I think he's expressing the illusion of a unified consciousness slowly unbraiding. Buddha got to a place where he qualitatively experienced what cognitive science thinks is true of the mind. My "I" as I meditate seems to be very much essentialized in my experiences. Without seeing a bunch of crap happen over and over again very dependably, I don't even know if I'd have an intuition of cause and effect. Which is where Hume and Buddha start to boogie together. And I can't help but feel that the particular crap I dependably saw is part of who I am. And it can never be recreated.

Does this seem foolish to you? Am I missing the point? Arguing sideways? Is my soul something deeper than my "I"? Then what is it?

(I use that word deliberately) between metaphors and reality that we can only dimly perceive in our world but becomes Platonic when we're without our bodies. There is some Catholic stuff I can't abide, like "come suffer the little children," having to pretend to be a perpetual child and not reasonable (I wanted to marry a rabbi and convert when I was little—because you could ask reasonable *questions* in Judaism) . . . and yet, when I dig back into my early Catholic mysteries and see what there is left for me to hold, maybe there is something about faith and childhood and a slippage through reason and a play between ideas that is all play. It is so hard for children to stop playing and so hard for adults to begin playing, and what if the afterlife is all play, and a place where love is not in the least disappointing.

But I mean, truly, Max, what do I know? I am trying to be wise for you but I too am behind a glass darkly. What about those two black holes colliding in space and the sound they made that scientists measured yesterday?

Hume always left me cold.

Only the ancients comfort me when it comes to these questions. Freud I'd like to send down a laundry chute sometimes, and Hume I only pretend to understand.

I do think it's all to do with love somehow.

I do think there is something bigger than the "I," and I do believe when we glimpse it there is a great deal of beauty. Where the consciousness of the ant meets the consciousness of the shrew and our own grasping little brains.

I understand what you say about Theseus and your little boat. But I do not believe you are only carrying a torch of fear into the night with you. You might think you are carrying a torch of fear, Max, but what I see you holding is a torch of incredible luminosity, bravery, generosity to all of those around you, and metaphysical HEART. Big, big, big! Good, good, good! Bright, bright, bright! Illuminating the way in front of you and imparting light to the people you love.

Super Why is now over. "Solving some super big mysteries. Can the super readers save the day?" is wafting from the adjoining room to me. It means—I must feed Hope lunch.

I will write more soon. Thank you for your dear letter, and for your dear enormous heart.

Love,
Sarah

P.S. Now my three kids are asleep and my quasi-rabbinical husband is reading the *New York Times*. So I have a moment to write an addendum. My anecdote about Harry Potter World was perhaps a bad analogy for the afterlife because it implies that what's necessary to cheer the children is participation in an illusion. And that we are all frightened or upset children in need of an illusion to protect us from our wet pants. And I suppose what I'm suggesting is that what might seem illusory on this side is irrelevant on the other side. That reason is a wormhole and illusion is itself an illusion through which we wriggle. Wittgenstein's ladder . . . Pascal's wager . . . perhaps we are protected in this life from any knowledge of the other side in order to have the utmost freedom to invent our own faith. This is all sounding terribly Catholic and not very Buddhist at all. Testing theories with reason—that is what the rational Buddhist does. Maybe that is why I'm interested in Tibetan Buddhism, because it's the closest I can get to my childhood faith—it too has people who disappear inside caves after a week, leaving only traces of fingernails and hair—only Tibetan lamas purport to have done such things many times, and in this century too. Probably I am making no sense.

Your question about identity—is there a deeper substratum of identity than the "I" with which we identify? In Buddhism it is the subtle body, in Catholicism it is the soul. But the concept of *soul* involves more personality perhaps than the little seed or germ in Buddhism that gets to be passed on. Neither, I think, is greatly affected by the shaping of the personae or personality in the psychoanalytic sense. They are immutable and eternal and distinct from ego. I suppose I have always insisted on believing in the soul—even when that belief is at variance with my other philosophical or metaphysical beliefs. It just seems right. Look at that soul of yours, after all! Positively radiant!

And enough of the eschatology . . . it is all so abstract, and again, what do I know anyway? The main thing is that I'm thinking of you a great deal, and wondering how you are feeling and what you are doing. I had a dream that you stopped chemotherapy. Are you still on it and is it making you tired? Are you still sitting in your remarkable chair? Is Victoria there, and what is she doing?

I am coming to Los Angeles on April 7 and would love to see you then.

Lots of love,
Sarah

Sarah,

April would be wonderful, if I am in Los Angeles, which is likely. The only other place I could be is (can you believe it?) Israel, for a clinical trial. The drug on trial blasts mice free of Ewing's tumors even if they're in the bone. Bone tumors are usually the most difficult to wipe out, because the bones don't drink much of whatever poison you put into your blood.

Wouldn't it be great if my cure was in Israel? I think it would be a hilarious counterpoint to Hitler's life—for the descendant of Holocaust survivors to use Rothschild-esque connections to fly to an ultranationalist Jewish state in the Middle East to receive exclusive cancer treatment. I'm really the anti-Holocaust—far too many resources being wasted to save one little Jew . . .

I love that Peter Pan play so much—I can't wait to see Hook killed on stage and then brought back to life. And all just because the kids are impulsive. Impulsive mercy. Maybe that's what's at the heart of play.

But impulsive mercy is for William and me and you, and not for worms. Don't worry—I got the Harry Potter sermon immediately. I know William is much more a wizard than he is a butterbeer-besotted boy. I get that that's realer. I get that play is everywhere, and everything. It's just not nothing. It's never nothing. And I worry death is nothing.

As for our "I"—when I worried that experiences are part of the "I," I meant experiences in the most primitive of ways (just this one time, it was you and not me who brought Freud into this!). I meant experiences as basic as light hitting the eye. Like how kitty cats need light to hit their eyes in the first few days or they are blind for life. That changes their "I," I think. If you don't have triangles, or the color green, it changes what visions you have—it changes the dreams, metaphors—the portals to the afterlife. If you go Full Plato, I suppose there are Forms of Triangles and Green and all that stuff the kitten doesn't get through her eyes. But I can't buy it.

But maybe to atomize like this is to miss the point you're making. Of course there are souls. There's no denying the soul—it's too fiercely a useful thing, a bafflingly useful thing. You can look at mine. I can look at yours. We feel love, which is all we've ever wanted. Knowing your soul lets me miraculously predict what food you'd like to eat, and which chair you'll sit in, in what weather. That's really insane, given how many foods and chairs there are—it'd take an impossibly fancy computer to figure that out on a case-by-case basis, without having your soul software installed. Every person, whether they like it or not, has unshakable faith in souls, or they'd never be able to interact with anyone else. The fluency in the world and in one another that the soul endows us with . . . there's some Plato magic in that I *can* buy. (Or perhaps some Wittgenstein magic—since the soul's meaning and truth and apparency, as I see it, comes from unignorable usefulness. Which is just how W. thought language worked. Which is unlike Plato, who thought language and souls were True on their own terms.)

Perhaps, Sarah, souls are in the eye of the beholder. What if the soul is no more than the success with which we envision one another? What if you make me and I make you, and we need each other to make each other? Couldn't that be beautiful? Maybe our impermanence makes our love all the fiercer—since we are each other's gods or artists. And we only get to be for as long as we—in particular—love one another? Again, I find myself bringing the afterlife and divinity back into contact with our blood and guts, with this particular moment in time.

Today, Dad and Victoria and I went to a burger joint. Everyone there wanted to talk. I innocently asked a man if my fallen onion ring, close to his hungry boxer, could be fed to the dog. After a sharp *"No!"* he started into the narrative of his dog's hard-won weight loss. I said his dog looked very athletic, and he lit up with a huge smile, right from his soul. This was the stuff of this man, and nothing could substitute for it.

I'm not gonna go quite Freud here, but I feel myself maybe taking a closer tack—maybe you read right through me, as you're wont to do. This man and his dog and their connection—there are people who are just as inextricably knotted into their houseplants. Their shoes. Trivial material things. If neurons don't seem like the staples of the soul, if it's love, then how can love be anything other than the things we're loving?

And some of the things we love here in life are gods. What about idols? The little plaster blue Buddha you mailed me, that is my Buddha, and my prayers go to *it*. If I prayed to another Buddha, I would not be worshipping the same god. *It is it—nothing else*—so very easy to see in plaster, so very hard to see in people. There can't be my soul without that Buddha. It has instructed my soul—a vine on any other trellis bears different fruit. And with the exception of some very lucky lamas who get handed their Articles of Reincarnation every time they hit age four, the rest of us—were we to go back into life—would do so never, ever to reunite with the plaster gods who we love, who we are.

I know I seem to be all Reason and no Faith. But to me, I am all Faith in *it is it*—and *it is it* requires massive leaps. There is no empiricism without the imagination. Reason just helps me develop my Faith in *it is it*. I don't see why the two were ever put against one another. They seem, so automatically, to want to bring out the best in one another.

Victoria is working on a charcoal next to me. It's a large landscape with a couple of figures in it—and her foliage has gotten too dense, and from a distance, it's all a gray smear. Perhaps she's an omen for our metaphysical quibbles. I am suggesting she wipe out the gray sky and much of the leaves and replace it with a geometric rug-like pattern full of stark white. She thinks if she does this it'll look amateurish. She wants to start anew, with a zoom-in on the figures. What do you think she should do? Perhaps her solution will point to a metaphysical answer. Or, at least, it will replace our two imaginations, fruitfully colliding, with a coimagination. And, all the better, a coimagination *with her*. It takes two to tango, but you step all over one another's feet when you tango. Three on the other hand—three's a charm. Which is just what our faith needs. Three's also a very stable tricycle, which is much more rational than a bike. In any case, I'll keep you updated on her charcoal.

I love you. Scans tomorrow. You will know within minutes. I will try to be a brave carriage for the wormhole inside me, plugged up though it is with goopy little lumps. I am so happy to be in paradox with you. Not anti-dox—just para-, just beliefs alongside.

Whoever is right, I just realized, we both win. We'll always know one another forever, however long ever is. And that's all I want—is to know you forever.

Max

Dearest Max,

I love your dear letter. Let's know each other forever!

I will write a longer letter later because I have to go teach.

But quickly . . .

One funny thought I had when you said "W." for "Wittgenstein" was that you meant W. as in George Bush and I thought, "Wow, did Bush think that about language?"

Also—was your use of the word "tricycle" purposeful? (Buddhism being the vehicle and the wheels being three pronged?)

Why do we ride bicycles instead of tricycles in adulthood? They say the triangle is the most stable shape but my three children seem quite rickety sometimes in terms of constantly toppling each other over.

"I'm afraid death is nothing." But we've never found nothing! We can't find nothing anywhere! It requires such a leap of faith to believe in nothing! I've never seen nothing anywhere! Not even those black holes talking to each other in space are nothing, properly speaking. No matter where I look I can't find it! Emptiness, maybe; nothing, never.

And you're right—I falsely injected the straw man of Freud into the conversation. I thought first that that was what you meant about childhood conditioning our adult personalities. You meant more Proust than Freud. Another question: can souls have preferences? Or are souls beyond preference?

And the twin towers of faith and reason—perhaps their parallel coexistence is what is meant by nondualism . . . oh, there is so much to be said, and it makes my brain hurt.

I love the idea that you might go to the Holy Land to get your tumors blasted away. But I hope you are not in the Holy Land while I am in Los Angeles. We would be surrounded by palm trees on opposite ends of the earth!

There is so much more to say—about totems and athletic dogs and Victoria's charcoal drawing! Please send her my love. I am so glad she is with you—I have to say, you have sounded much better since she has arrived.

More as I know it, or at least wonder about it . . .

Lots of love, and fingers crossed on scan day,
Sarah

That February, scan day was not a good day. There were multiple new metastases in the lung and lymph nodes. To cheer Max up, his mother arranged for a quick trip for him and Victoria to San Francisco, where they spent a weekend trying to forget. They were still newlyweds, married five months. Max called me and went into rhapsodies describing the pizza they ate there. And he sent me this poem:

EARTHQUAKE COUNTRY BEFORE FINAL CHEMOTHERAPY

For the first time tonight,
as I put my wife to bed
I didn't have to shove her off me.

She turned away in her sleep.·

I wondered what was wrong with my chest.

I felt myself, and the collarbone
spiked up and where she'd rest
her cheek was ribs.

Who wants to cuddle a skeleton?

My skeleton wandered from the house
and out onto the street.

He came, after much wandering, to the edge of a bay
where a long bridge headed out—
the kind that hangs itself with steel

and sways as if the wind could take
away its weight.

There were mountains in the distance—
triangles of cardboard—
or perhaps the mist was tricking his eyes.

The instant the mist made him doubtful,
it turned to rain.

The rain covered everything. The holes in
his face were so heavy
he wondered if the water was thickening—
if he was leaching into them.

He panicked. Perhaps he was gunked up
with that disgusting paste,
flesh, all over again.

When his last wish
was an instant in the sun
all to himself—

like a child gripping a too-big
beach ball with his whole body

before exploding to the sand,
the ball hurtling to the sun.

If I were alive I'd have told him
I was nothing like what he was feeling—

that the rain felt more like
the shell of a crab
than the way I'd held him.

That it felt more like *him*.

But I wasn't alive—
I was the ghost in the bridge
willing the cars to join me,

telling them that death was not wind,
was not weight,

was not mist,
and certainly not the mountains—

that it was the breaking apart,

the penetration of all forms of life and earth
with one another.

That it was replacement of *Who*, *When*, *How*, and *Where*
questions
with *What* questions.

When my skeleton looked down
he was corrupted
in the femur by fracture,
something swelling within.

Out of him leaked pink moss.
Water took it away.

Dearest Max,

What a beautiful poem. I adore it. The image of the skeleton walking by himself to the bridge. I want to reread it many times. There is something beautifully Japanese about it. I love so much:

Who wants to cuddle a skeleton?

My skeleton wandered from the house
and out onto the street.

Last night I dreamed I was in Los Angeles driving around (of course what else is there to do but drive around there) and William wasn't in the car, he was walking, and I was worried for him walking down big highways by himself, and I was going to meet you and Victoria for dinner. I gave you a tremendous hug.

I think it was brilliant of you two to escape to San Francisco after your alarming news. Part of me wishes they would stop poking around and looking inside of you—like opening an oven door on something baking. I know that is naive of me medically—that they are trying to save you by looking inside of you. And that the something baking is not a nice something baking, but tumors they are trying to remove. But the anxiety of every test—and the cold peering in—and the waiting for news—I hate it all. And part of me wishes you could just be writing poems with no medical gaze to interrupt your daily life.

I am rereading *Middlemarch* with Tony. This sentence reminded me of you:

> To be a poet is to have a soul so quick to discern that
> no shade of quality escapes it, and so quick to feel that
> discernment is but a hand playing with finely-ordered
> variety on the chords of emotion—a soul in which
> knowledge passes instantaneously into feeling, and feel-
> ing flashes back as a new organ of knowledge.

I am SO GLAD Victoria took a leave from Princeton and is with you without interruption. Thank God. Did you guys drive up the coast? Are you going to double back through Big Sur? I hope that the ocean is blue enough. You both deserve the most blue ocean in your sights today.

xoxoox,
Sarah

The velocity of Max's writing at this time was staggering. He
sent me another poem the next day:

SELF-PORTRAIT AS JESUS

My hand let pain see.

My hand was a head
for an eye of red.

Pain saw a nail.

My other hand then,

and my chest slit with gills
for the new thing
taking over.

I abandoned my mind's garden
of my own accord.

I expected weeds, worms, moles,
but nothing like this—

the soil curdled into a lumpy ocean,
a flat fish eating a bottom
that's always eroding.

It stirs. I bleed. A lesson:
Pain is just panic sitting still a moment.

As my blood pours
it moves the air.

I feel all of you pulled
into the vacuum behind it, down my legs

to the brown ground.

Test your cells, hold them tight
in machines forever.
The white ones are saints,
the red ones are people.

I want you to know
I once had friends,

that I served them uncontrollably,
sometimes full of contempt. That this was grace.

Dearest Max,

Of course you knew my little Catholic heart would leap for a Jesus poem. It is very beautiful. I love the images of the hands seeing through an eye of pain, of the red and white blood cells as saints and people.

Last night Tony said in his sleep, reaching for the ceiling, "The future of mankind depends upon your curiosity!"

I might have to make a poem out of it.

Off to teach. How is chemo?

Xooo,
Sarah

Sarah—

Chemo is hard. I'm not on ifosfamide, which was the much-feared one with neurotoxicity. Turns out that ifos is actually derived from mustard gas. I'm on a guy named trabectedin, which is derived from sea squirts. I'm nauseous and very fatigued. I really wanna poo. Goji berries don't help. Only Fleets. And there's a limit to the number of Fleets one can reasonably do. I don't want a flotilla in there, making the Battle of Midway in my pants.

Sorry I was making Anna carsick with my voice earlier.

Love you,
Max

At this point, Max was sending out his work with a new urgency, and it seemed the right time for us to contemplate making a little book of our letters, as we'd discussed. One of my all-time favorite books when I was busy (or not busy) becoming a person was *Letters to a Young Poet*, by Rainer Maria Rilke. It occurred to me once I grew up and reread that book that it was a one-sided conversation; we never got to read the letters from the young poet. Maybe they were boring. Or maybe they didn't survive.

At any rate, Max and I published a sample of our letters on *Berfrois*, with a charming illustration by Victoria; child-like versions of me and Max sitting on a seesaw suspended over lapis bricks in space, floating by a planet or two. Now we were contemplating making a bigger book. I wanted Max to help shape the book while he still could. So I sent him a huge document of all our emails stitched together. All in all there were probably five hundred pages. But was it a book?

Max expressed worry that it would read either like a boring scholarly tome or "a Lifetime movie story of poor cancer boy and his wise, brilliant, loving mentor ministering to his heart and mind through every mortal peril and petty crisis." Max was disgusted by such narratives. His instinct was to select only our favorite twenty or so letters and make a slim volume. I wasn't so sure, arguing for more letters, more chronology. We kept going back and forth.

Meanwhile, Max was sending out *Four Reincarnations* with dogged, fevered hope. He sometimes got discouraged. Conversations, over the phone and by text, went like this:

MAX:

I don't think anyone wants my book.

SARAH:

A brilliant manuscript needs to be rejected at least twenty times before someone publishes it, you know that, right?

MAX:

I don't have time.

SARAH:

It will get published. I promise you.

✳

And then, glory be! Milkweed Editions agreed to publish his book.

One of Max's literary friends had sent the manuscript to Daniel Slager at Milkweed on a Friday; Daniel fell in love with the book over the weekend, and offered to publish the book on Monday. Max was determined to live at least until he could hold the book in his hands.

Hey Sarah, Sarah, O My Sarah,

This chemo has been hard to recover from. I've had so much of it over the years—my body just doesn't want to play the game anymore. I felt seasick and gagged and threw up and was bedridden and had no thoughts other than "Bbhuuhhhhh" for a week. I can now move around the house a bit—and walked to the market today to pick up French toast supplies with Victoria. She treated me to a sublime French toast with berry compote and orange-zested Greek yogurt. I am not myself. I miss being fluent in my body—I don't even know what stretches it needs. My muscles don't have cravings anymore. I love it when my muscles tell me that they want weight, or to really quickly fire. None of that right now. Elizabeth's wedding is in a couple of weeks, so I'm gathering strength for that. I need to write my sermon.

I have read through the draft of all the emails you've stitched together. Firstly: thanks so much for taking a first swipe. I am sorry I didn't get to it first. I've been so sick. Normally I'm able to think through and work through the sickness . . . but not right now. Maybe it's the round-the-clock OxyContin. The pills make me feel "better" in a way I don't like . . . I think they make me a little less desperate to survive. And work is survival, and so I haven't been working.

The letters made me really happy and sentimental.

I also must say: you were majorly patient in those early emails. I really just threw the gelatinous blob of neurosis that I was into your frying pan, looked up at you, and said "Let's get cooking!" within like a month of knowing you. Thanks for not getting freaked out by my oversharing. I'm sorry I talked about my poop so much when we were getting acquainted.

Also: thanks for dealing with my German-lit-crit/Gilbert and Sullivan writing style. I always associated that monstrous time in my writing with my freshman year, but my lord. It apparently took a long time to die. (I remember writing an analysis of my friend's Cinderella play in sophomore year for his playbill and an acquaintance remarking, "Gee . . . you sure know a lot of words . . ." I used "Apotropaic" in the title of the piece.) My father, when I was a little boy, told me that vocabulary was what separated man from beast, and Jew from Everyman, and High IQ from Republican. This took a long time to correct.

And some of those poems I wrote. Barf. But some of them. Not bad, past Max.

I am going to write to you next about Religions You're Born Into vs. Religions You're Drawn To—which I think is a more substantial distinction than any made between individual religions in terms of the spiritual significance or meaning of a religion to the soul. Don't think I've forgotten! But now I'm very fatigued. Maybe you can start us off a little. Tell me

again and in more detail about how your inherited Catholic
afterlife played against the Reincarnation you found and
loved.

Love, Love, L=o=v=e,
Max

Dearest Max,

That French toast sounds fucking good. I want some now. Hooray Victoria!

I'm so sorry this round of chemo was terrible and I'm hoping that you're almost out of the worst of it. The muscles not having cravings—somehow your description reminded me of that Wordsworth poem—the "glad animal movements all gone by."

One thing I find hilarious is how hard you are on yourself—on your writer-self or otherwise. I would be the last to notice a tendency towards swollen words. A poem I wrote in fourth grade went something like this: "Prisoner of a prodigy . . . prattling prolix profusely . . ." There are some good things about growing up. Word-size moderation, for one.

But on a deeper level—I would not have judged your writing in that way, Max. It was *you*! Not words. I saw YOU, Max! Not the word-building architecture, which is a part of you, of course.

I'm in Louisville still with the Peter Pan play. Had a run-through the other night in which I thought, "Oh, I've written a play that goes like this—section one: depressing, section two: boring, section three: weird." But I think it was just the agony of moving from the intimacy of the rehearsal room into the exposure of the theater, and technical details of flying still being in everyone's head. I like rehearsals in the room best. I could take or leave the whole audience-coming part.

So yes—I want to read your thoughts about chosen religions and inherited ones. I love your thought that inherited religions (no matter the dogma) have more in common with each other than with chosen religions. I had a stray thought about another good topic yesterday—what was it? Oh, yes, dreams. What the hell are they? I thought Victoria could help here. Sometimes I have a memory of the feeling of a dream—a trace impression—it's so vivid—I can remember an image from the dream, and the experience of being in it—and then it's gone—and it's often a dream from years ago that wasn't terribly significant. What *is* that? And what does it mean for embodiment and consciousness?

Hope that you're gaining strength, and writing your sermon. Where is Elizabeth getting married? Please pass my congratulations on to her.

Lots of love,
Sarah

Max presiding at the wedding of his dear friend, the poet Elizabeth Metzger.

Subject: Heavens are all alike, the people who make them are all artists

S'ardent-arah,

Today was slow. Victoria and I took a short walk on San Vicente. We like taking mindful walks, both together and on our own, where we just sort of get as involved in the surroundings as possible. We notice the subway vibrating underfoot and the way it's in tune with a window being shut on the street. We've both remarked in the past that San Vicente is a really hard street to do this on. That Los Angeles in general is hard for mindful walks. So much space occupied by sky and so many identical beige banks. But today we found a trick. We sat on a ledge near a traffic light and looked into cars. And this made mindfulness really easy and engaging again. So many people, dressed so funnily, doing such strange things with their mouths. A mountain of a man tucked in a three-piece suit drove a black Cadillac Escalade (a chauffeur in Los Angeles?!). A balding millennial Jew listened to gangster rap in his Prius with his windshield wipers blasting away in the bone-dry seventy-degree air.

A few days ago you told me a story. The pills I'm on are corrupting my memory, so I'll probably screw this up. But the story was, basically, that you were discussing the afterlife with a Tibetan Buddhist. You told her that you were bowled over by how comforting reincarnation seems. And she told you she'd always felt reincarnation was sort of blah . . . just more of the same *and*, to boot, you can get lost in the underworld—stuck in strange hells for eternity for the silliest and most arbitrary reasons. She thought the Catholic heaven you grew up with—now *THAT* was comforting. You asked if I hadn't been alarmed growing up with no afterlife. And I said, "Eh."

And I said that the differences between afterlives are pretty negligible in terms of their spiritual meaning. (I'm a bit Baha'i.) But the difference, to the spirit, of the afterlife you are born into, on the one hand, and the afterlife you later meet and perhaps choose, on the other—that THAT was real. And that all the Born Religions have some common feeling to them, and all the Chosen Religions have some common feeling to them. I said I thought Catholicism-for-your-Buddhist-friend and Tibetan-Buddhism-for-you have a deep kinship.

So now I'll explain myself, as you asked me to do. So first off: how can I pretend, for a second, that there's no difference between the different afterlives? That a forever of earths is no different than eternal Jesus Woodstock or the vague Jewish promise that you and God will be together and, more importantly, definitely not not-together like the goyim will be? How are all these answers to "Where do we go" the same?

Here's what I think: I think the question is so good that we begin to think of the answers in a special way. Where the answers are all Good in the most profound and deepest sense. And thus there can be no wrong answer. Stay with me:

You know when you encounter a sentence or even a word in a poem that it is—by virtue of being in a poem—special. That you're supposed to think about it differently. That it isn't there to be dismissed. Or taken at face value. That it isn't even there to be argued with. That it's there to be unlocked, or perhaps never unlocked. That it is there to be studied.

And study, as you've taught me, is secular worship. Let's imagine a poem that opens, "Close the door." I think of how daring it is to start crisply with a command, that the first thing we hear is a command (like if a Bible started with "Let there be light"). I think that the poem might be forcing me into intimacy with it by shutting off the rest of the world when it invites me to close the door—that once the door is closed, I am at the mercy of this voice. I think of how the verb *close* (as in "close the door") could also be the adjective *close* (as in "hold me close")—that by closing the door I'm getting close to the voice. That closure and closeness and intimacy and demand are deliciously tangled up in one another. The only thing I *don't* think is to physically get up and close the door of my room.

If a religion writes a text about the afterlife, it is always, always asking that the text be read as a poem. The question "What is the afterlife?" is so beautiful, so profound, so rich, that any response demands respect. That response becomes as rich as the imagination of the person reading the response.

The phrase "Close the door" is just the first one that came to mind, but it could answer the question "What is the afterlife?" in a way that would be lovely. The question "What is the afterlife?" is a metaphorical museum around the ready-made urinal of "Close the door." Zen Buddhism does stuff much stranger and pithier and Dada. "What is the afterlife?" is a framing device that expects the best of us—that already engages with such unimpeachably deep and lovely components of the human spirit that we can't but smile and do our best for it. When we ask about the afterlife, we're conquering death with imagination. We're making our loved ones go on forever. We're saying that we're having so much fun, we don't want it to ever stop. Or if it does stop, we want to know the rest of the exciting date that's planned. What could be better in people than wanting to know this? When you say "What is the afterlife?" I think you are assuming humans are good. (And I hope poems assume the same. And every time I write a poem, I embarrassingly and perhaps delusionally imagine strangers kind enough to listen to the poem respectfully. And this is the most romantic and optimistic I can be. Maybe many poets are liberals because they have to assume people are good in order to assume that people will want to read and worship their poems. And liberals tend to assume people are good. Let's have a separate conversation on that.)

So it doesn't matter if it's reincarnation Sarah close-reads into meaning. Or the Catholic heaven that her friend does. The main thing is that it's something that you chose to play with—*to imagine into*. And more than that, you imagined your soul into it. Jesus Christ, Sarah—how much more respectful can you be? You *trusted your life* to reincarnation. You *gave your life* to it. Your friend did the same with Catholicism. They're both lurid, gorgeous tapestries. But the color comes from your essence, which dyes the fibers.

No answer to the question of the afterlife remains the same as itself for an instant. No two Christians have envisioned heaven identically or even, I think, very similarly. As soon as a new human being touches a doctrine, as soon as they start amplifying certain parts of it, dimming others, it is altered. That's why you didn't even notice the hells in which one gets lost in Tibetan reincarnation. And why your friend, if I can conjecture, didn't think about how boring being happy all the time would be at Jesus Woodstock. And immersion in a doctrine, far from helping you have an objective under-standing of it, makes things even WORSE! Think about two literary critics who've spent their lives with *Hamlet* and how ludicrously more divergent their understandings of the play are than those of a couple of sixth-graders cutting their teeth on it for the first time. The religions that have stuck around contain their opposites many times over. Jesus is all merciful and then all of a sudden, if you don't love him, you're gonna be cut from the tree and withering and dying. Zen Buddhism is an entire religion about contradicting itself.

Louise once told me she loves contradictory adages like "Distance makes the heart grow fonder" and "Out of sight, out of mind." I asked her, "But which is true?" And she said, "They appear exactly when we need them, and in that moment there is no denying their truth." I think religions are similar—presenting us with the unimpeachable right when we need it, and willing, like a protective Jewish mother, to revise the past or self-contradict to protect our hearts and our present tenses.

But no matter what afterlife someone chooses, choosing an afterlife has the same baptism. You ask the answer of the questions. You read the afterlife like a poem.

I suppose this can apply to the afterlife you're born with—but it's not a *necessary* component to it. That afterlife can just sort of be there. You form your relationship to it before you ever learn how to read poems. And you don't *have* to ever learn to read it like a poem. In this way, all afterlives you're born with are similar.

To choose a religion is to fall in love with God. And it's hard to fall in love with something you're born in love with. Oh no—Freud is begging me to go Oedipal here but I promise I'll leave it.

But I will say: your family gives you your first afterlife. Your family gives you the texts. But humanity offers you your next afterlife. You encounter your next afterlife because you encounter other human beings. You get to think, "Wow—human beings have endured for millions of years with this heaven, or this system to get back on earth. And since I have empathy, and since I feel things deep in my heart that I know to be true, I can have this system too." And chance, too, offers you your next afterlife. You stumble on it by meeting the right person or reading the right book. And chance is, however fictionally, Fate. And Fate is a palpable expression of the divine just for you. It's a miracle for no one else. Just for you.

There's also something painfully earnest and a bit sad when people read their childhood afterlives as poems. They always know that deep down there's an earlier and simpler draft of things. Maybe they miss that draft. Even if they don't—there's the lingering suspicion that that was where the wisdom was. The kind of clarity I had as a kid, however false it was, never really left me as feeling like the "right way" for the world to be. Adult Max is much subtler and more graceful, but I'm so harried by worry that I sometimes think, "Well, it all seemed so right before I had complicated opinions . . . so maybe it was?"

I find poets who never converted and who write venerative poetry a bit awkward and sad. "Poor sad Hopkins . . . what a weirdo," I think. Or simply, "Herbert . . . what a weirdo." I love these guys, but I cringe a bit imagining them as human beings going to the store or reading the newspaper. It's like they're trying to cram their very adult bodies into their communion robes. Is it possible to write about a childhood religion without writing about your family? When I write about my family, I have to be pretty self-aware. (In fact, I write about Judaism, but it's always self-aware to the point of self-mockery.) I don't want to *have* to be self-aware, though, for poetry like this. I want it to be ecstatic. Now there are exceptions. Julian of Norwich. Saint Augustine. But those people were so imaginative that they basically made new religions. I don't see much of their first religion at all anymore. I think this is the way to do it—wipe out all that you knew and use your heart and head to do it all from scratch.

And Sarah: all this from someone with no *belief* in the afterlife at all! Is that a problem? Is it silly to say there's nothing nobler than having a poem-like afterlife when I don't have a belief in one? I feel like I get to have all the afterlives, because I don't have to believe in any one but I try to understand them all. I think belief is overrated. Understanding is much, much more important. I feel like on Judgment Day, Jesus wouldn't ask, "Did you truly believe?" but "Did you truly understand?" And I would say, "Yes!" and give him a big hug. Belief is yucky. It's somehow very secular seeming and gauche to me. Like it's about predictive powers. Weathermen come to mind. And poker. It's like God is hiding the dice and we have to guess the numbers on it correctly. And one day we'll guess. And then the party is over. I guess if I believed in an afterlife, I'd one day find out if I was right or not, and from that moment on, I couldn't write the poem of the afterlife anymore. I'd have to stop playing. You know how you talked about William's wizarding pants and play?

Belief, I think, responds to fear. When I imagine people *believing* really hard in the afterlife I imagine them white-knuckled with fear and going, "No don't worry I'm going to heaven I'm going to heaven I'm going to heaven." But trying to understand the afterlife, that seems to come from a place of compassion, of benign curiosity. Understanding is play for me. The game of understanding is always changing its own rules, just like Calvinball. Scientists wonder and they don't do it for any reason other than that it feels deeply right to wonder. I think that's why I love scientists. Play and science are two of the only human activities that don't seem to have much of an agenda to them. That don't involve manipulating or coercing or any kind of violence. And that are willing to go, "Oh, never mind . . . guess I was wrong . . . let's look over here."

Speaking of which. Victoria just bolted up in bed and said "hi" and then she went back to sleep. I think she's having a dream that she wants me to come play in. Or perhaps help her do some science in. So I'm going to sleep and catch her mid-dream and do some playing.

Never insult a potato,
Max

Dear teacher Max,

What a wonderful letter to wake up to. So much so that to answer it point by point would be useless—it's only: I agree. And yes. And I'm so glad you're strong enough now to take walks with Victoria! Please send her my love.

What you say is a comfort. If all poetry and all religions are addressing this basic human design flaw—we are born, we fall in love with life and other people, and then we die—then the persistence of love appears to me to be the most important salve. Death wouldn't be so awful if you could bring love along with you. And most poetry and most religion says that love triumphs over death. Buddhism doesn't talk about love that much, or at least not with that nomenclature. I wonder if that's a translation issue. The word *compassion* appears rather than *love*. Being born into the cauldron of the Judeo-Christian world, it's love I'm more interested in, ultimately . . . I can't help myself.

If we didn't love in this lifetime, life would be hell on earth. And yet it makes the leaving of it more difficult, if you can't bring love along with you. Maybe that's why Buddhists re-name some love attachment, to soften the blow. Or maybe I am missing the point, which is that you can't bring attach-ment along with you, but you always have love, that's the ground upon which all else sits.

But your subject line, "Heavens are all alike, the people who make them are all artists," seems unimpeachable to me.

The story about my Buddhist friend's exposure to Catholicism went like this . . . and it came from my babysitter Yangzom, who will be a Tibetan Buddhist until the end or longer . . . she said that one time there was a Catholic who was dying in her village in Tibet. And the Catholic was singing prayers to heaven and seemed very calm and happy. And Yangzom was impressed, as a child, watching this dying Catholic, for to her, a young Buddhist, death was fraught with peril and fear—various hells and the possibility that you might come back as a cockroach. Whereas this Catholic thought they only had to confess and be forgiven and they'd go straight to heaven. And this interested me because somehow reincarnation seemed to me (the latecomer) much more comforting than the dichotomy of heaven and hell.

You mention Julian of Norwich, who said, "Know it well, love was God's meaning. Who reveals it to you? Love. What did God reveal to you? Love. Why does God reveal it to you? For love. Remain in this, and you will know more of the same. And you will never know different, without end." This was read at my wedding by our friend Danya Ruttenberg, a writer and bisexual crusader for gender equity who became a conservative rabbi and moved to Israel and married a man and had three children—she is quite an astonishing person. (And Julian of Norwich had a mystic conversion, didn't she? And Saint Augustine too. So they fit right into your model, distinguishing themselves from Herbert and Hopkins—your thoughts on whom made me laugh out loud.)

So if God is love and poetry is love and neither have bodies so both can triumph over death, then we can bring love with us to all of our heavens, which are all alike.

When I taught my children about reincarnation, I think it might have had the opposite effect from what I intended, which was comfort, when their grandmother died. At least Anna was not comforted but alarmed by the thought that I might come back one day in a different form and she wouldn't be able to recognize me. Better to keep me in heaven with my selfhood intact, and meet me later. She said to me, "Mom, promise me that you'll come back and be my child and I'll be able to recognize you." Anna herself thinks she might be a reincarnation of my father . . . speaking of . . .

My father once wrote this letter to me, which I've always kept with me as a talisman and I'll close with. My father's last letter to me was this:

> Joseph Ferdinand Gould, self-styled "Last of the Bohemians," slept on park benches, in hallways and subways, and was occasionally picked up for vagrancy. Joe also wrote poetry. His verse was terse, viz—

>> In winter I'm a Buddhist,
>> And in summer I'm a nudist.

With this couplet, Joe became a member of the Raven
Poetry Society of Greenwich Village, though not without opposition. He was accused of not being serious
enough, whereupon he retorted that neither were most
of its members, since they wrote only on such "trite
themes as life, love and death." Supported enthusi-
astically by Maxwell Bodenheim, Joe was admitted.
He immediately translated a poem by his sponsor
into "seagull," a language Joe claimed to know. This
offended everyone. "screek-squack—screek" went
the translation, with Joe making appropriate gestures
to impersonate a gull, and he was ejected. Cummings
wrote a poem one night after a walk. He started up
West Tenth Street, and saw "a little person who now is
dead and who lived by begging." He had known this
man well; but now he suddenly saw him as "someone
else." It was Joe Gould.

> walking in the dark
> i met christ
> jesus)my heart
> flopped over
> and lay still

Last week you and I were talking about one of
the trite themes identified by Joe Gould—love.
Cummings had some nice words to say on this subject. Years later, when a publisher decided to issue a
selection of George Herriman's panels, Cummings

was asked to write the introduction. He wrote it with love, and love is his theme.

> A lot of people "love" because, and a lot of
> people "love" although, and a few individuals
> love. Love is something illimitable; and a lot of
> people spend their limited lives trying to prevent
> anything illimitable from happening to them.

I'm humble that you have provided illimitable love to me. I hope you realize that my love for you is also illimitable. Whatever happens in the crazy twistings and turnings of my current situation, I know I can fall back on the love between us as one of the rocks in my life. Continue to grow and mature into womanhood. You have much to contribute to the world—I am only grateful that I've been one of the beneficiaries. You will always be in my thoughts this semester, and I look forward to spending the summer (maybe as Buddhists) with you pondering ("love thou art frail") why some love can be illimitable.

Hey Sarah,

I'm sorry I haven't written. My health fell apart the past couple of weeks from the chemo. I was sleeping upright in a chair from the nausea, and didn't leave my bed except to go to chemo, and was wheeled there and back. It was the worst I've been since 2008. I'm starting to come to.

Today is the anniversary of Melissa's death. I did a *metta* meditation on a self-portrait she painted.

Do you Tibetan Buddhists have metta? You go round three different faces you picture in your head. You start with a face you love—*cough*—sorry, I mean "have positive feelings toward." (You know how Zen is . . .) I use you often. Then after a few minutes you move to a face that's relatively neutral—like a grocery store clerk you saw that day, or John Kasich. Then you move on to someone you have a "complicated and turbulent relationship with." For me this is almost invariably an ex. As you look at each face you recite, "I wish you peace, I wish you happiness, I wish you freedom from internal and external harm." I sometimes add "however you define it." The idea is that your natural compassion toward someone you love can teach you how to offer compassion to those you're having trouble with.

It was so strange to do metta for a dead person. My first thought was: well, she's certainly more peaceful now than when I knew her and she was terrified of dying. And she's definitely not gonna be internally or externally harmed. Unless her bones count as her, because maybe they're being hurt by soil or bugs.

But happiness: how on earth can a dead person be happy? Or are dead people always happy? I thought about when I'm happiest. It usually means nothing is going wrong in my head, that I'm not anxious about anything. Life is pleasant when you're not anxious, sort of all on its own. If you're not anxious and there's a wall in front of you, you think, "Nice wall," and the creamy beige of the wall just sort of flows through you like vanilla ice cream. And that's, I think, what Buddha was talking about when he said desire causes all suffering. Because anxiety is always a form of desire— "I want this to go away, if only I had this, if only this were different."

But is happiness just a negative state? I know there's ecstasy and joy, but I don't think that's what you're supposed to wish someone in metta. Actually, I think most of my ecstasy is just me realizing "Oh shit, I'm really happy," and getting overwhelmed with how rare and strange that is. I remember one time teaching Victoria how to crab walk in our apartment. And then I realized it'd been a good hour or two without an anxious thought. There hadn't been any intrusive need to change where I was in the world, or who I was with. There were no tormenting memories of shameful things I'd done or people who'd wronged me. And I thought, "Oh shit . . . I'm really happy." And then I threw her on the couch and showered her with kisses and started weeping and wailing with ecstasy.

Teacher, what is happiness? Is it just getting out of your own way so the world can give you all its miracles? But do you have to be around to receive those miracles? What part of me is happy, if it seems the more I try and the more I am, the less happiness there is? I miss my dead friend, but I think she is more at peace. Could she be happier too?

I wrote a poem tonight. It's attached. Melissa is there, in a little line. I wish I knew more about her, and had had more time with her. I don't know the way to grieve properly.

I liked using metta—customs are toeholds on the sheer cliff of life. That's a paraphrase from the book *The End of Days*, which I just read, and which I'll mail to you. I think you'll like it.

Can't wait to see you. When is your Los Angeles trip again? I'm going to give you a bigger hug than you bargained for.

Max

THE OTHER BIRTHDAY

Perhaps where I am going, time is more
like itself: composed.

On this planet, I have a clipping of hair
and a twig with me,
in a warm room.

I say or think *I loved her, I hated him*
again and again, to stand in
for all the time spent
in the company of other people.

My memory can't reach beyond these phrases—
it's like sticking a twig into a tarp
and under the tarp is a sea
in which someone drowns.

Come to the room. I sometimes pretend the hair
is mine, and make the most outrageous noises
to mock the planet outside the room.

The twig is to help the drowning people
but they never know—
they just feel something urging them deeper,
deeper,

out of the room, back to the lovely planet
full of hooks and plugs
fit just right for their soft hands.

I want to believe you.
That the room is the threshold—
that's why it's warm.
That I'll meet Melissa soon.

But I'm pissing out my torn-up muscles.
Fluid is going where it shouldn't:
the lung, the space between the lip and nose, my PJs.

As I lie in bed, every new thought excites me
because I can't yet rule out
that it's the thing right before sleep.

Dearest Max,

It sounds like you have been through hell. I am so impressed you are able to write at all, and also to practice metta. Tibetan Buddhists do metta too—it's not dissimilar from tonglen.

You ask if the dead are happy. And you ask what is happiness.

I think the poets know better what happiness is than the philosophers do. Charlie Brown's friend says: Happiness is a warm blanket. Sei Shonagon has a list of things that give her pleasure, including piecing back together a letter that someone has torn up and thrown away, and finding she can read line after line in it. She also has pleasure when someone she loves is praised by others, or when someone she loves and who is far away is taken ill and news arrives that the illness has taken a turn for the better. And she says, "When a poem that you've composed for some event . . . is talked of by everyone and noted down when they hear it. This hasn't yet happened to me personally, but I can imagine how it would feel."

I suppose pleasure is of a different category than happiness. You are speaking in your happy story of freedom from care, freedom from worry. Equanimity? What I love about Buddhism is their happiness technology.

Things That Make Me Happy: when I wake from a nap and the light on my walls is bright with daylight. When my husband's eyes are alight with something he finds funny. When my children crawl into my bed and lie on top of me. When an old friend calls and I putter around and do the dishes while catching up with them. Swimming. Early magnolia trees in March. A perfectly brewed cup of tea. Letters from you, Max!

You ask if the dead are happy. I think some dead people are happy, and some are not, and some go on to be people again and have various degrees of happiness. Did I ever tell you the story of seeing a Korean acupuncture master? He specialized in physiognomy. He took one look at my face and said, "Father, father, father, I get nothing from you but your father. What does your father do?" "He's dead," I said. "Ah," he said, "lie down. You have to let your father go." And I thought, "No no no no! I Won't Let Him Go." I lay down on the table and he inserted a needle near my heart. I wept. The Korean acupuncturist said, "Now meditate every day for forty days on your father, to let him go. If you do not let him go, he will not have a good reincarnation, he will stay attached to this world." This was six years after my father had died. At that time I still carried a little piece of his handwriting around with me whenever I traveled. I thought of his handwriting like a code. I thought the letters might take me to him if I died. Did you know that in Tibetan metaphysics you are supposed to meditate on the Tibetan syllable *A* at the time of death in order to reach enlightenment? I think it's so interesting, the idea that a letter, a worldly letter, is thought to have the power to crack a metaphysical code. A prominent lama gave Thomas Merton this teaching on his travels to Asia, and Merton died shortly thereafter, electrocuted by a hair dryer. Some speculate that the lama foresaw his untimely death—and therefore gave him an esoteric teaching that would normally have been kept secret.

But are the dead happy? I used to imagine my father growing up in death, starting as a baby, and growing; three years after his death I imagined that he was in preschool, and I was his mother, having to drop him off at the door, having to let go. I was suffering as he happily went to explore counting beads. I think he is happy now. I used to listen to music he loved and it brought me suffering; now I listen to music he loved and it makes me happy. That makes me think he is happy.

The kids are clamoring for dinner. I should go. I am flying to Los Angeles Thursday! See you very soon.

Wishing you relief from the nausea and all the awfulness of chemo . . .

Love,
Sarah

I was able to visit Max several times that spring. I was in California on my annual pilgrimage to see my in-laws with the whole family, and I took the sleepy Amtrak train from Santa Barbara to Los Angeles to see Max. He would doze from morphine, then wake up, alert and ready for good conversation.

On one occasion, I was recounting to him a giraffe birth I'd seen at the Santa Barbara Zoo. Giraffe births are extraordinary. The baby giraffes fall from such a height! Max countered with his knowledge of marsupial births. Max, his mother, his wife, and I all gathered around a computer to watch a kangaroo get born. It gave rise to this small poem:

MARSUPIAL BIRTHS
For Max, Victoria, and Ari

1.

Today we four watched
a marsupial get born.

Red, tiny, covered with—what?
It climbs out its mother,
nothing more than a fetus, grafts itself to her fur,
burrows by smell into her pouch,
there to grow.

Two births for one small kangaroo.

You, Max, waiting, in the pouch of your steamer chair,
holding your red hot-water bottle,
which you call your second Max.

2.

When I gave birth I thought—oh—
death in reverse.
The pain, and the pushing yourself
outside your own body,
no longer your mother's
into some other dark pouch.

There to rest, there to think,
small and red and quiet.

So much courage to get born or die—
those giraffes dropping from the
great rooftops of their mothers' bodies—
learning to stand on the ground.

We are kangaroos—
finding our way into the dark
matted fur of our mothers' bodies.
And then the second birth—
peering out into the world.

On that trip, I did one last public reading of poetry with Max in a big, empty, light-filled room in Los Angeles. Max was too sick to read many of his own poems, so he asked me to read some for him. I read Max's poem "Hi, Melissa," one of my favorites. And Max read his poem "The Final Voicemails."

HI, MELISSA

I have spoken to you of heaven—
I simply meant the eyes are suns that see.
Seeing is the faces' nervous delicious Lord.

Listening to you makes me naked.
When I kiss your ankle I am silencing an oracle.
The oracle speaks from the hill of your ankle.

THE FINAL VOICEMAILS

1

I was told my proximity
to the toxin would promote
changes to my thinking, speech, and behavior.

My first thought was, of course,
for the child, the little girl,

but graceful, silent figures
in white suits flitted to her

and led her away by the shoulders, like two friends
taking a turtle from a pond.

My second thought was about pain,
the last thing visible
without our manners—

Or could there be an invisible peace
once the peace of the senses departs?

2

I'm glad she's gone, and not just for her sake:
without her I feel somehow better equipped
to be what I am becoming—

which is, I suppose, preoccupied.

Nobody ever tells you how *busy* loneliness is—

Every night I cover the windows in soap,
and through the night I dart
soap over any lick of light
that makes its way to my desk
or bed or the floor.

At first it was fear—an understanding that the light
was death, was the toxin,
though really the toxin was invisible,
they said, and came from the water.

But work blesses fear
like a holy man blessing a burlapped sinner,
saying *It is for you* and *Because of you,*

and in time the working mind
knows only itself, which is loneliness.

3

Dim sight now,
and each twitch flows
into a deep, old choreography.

Maybe a week ago, my arm banged the faucet,
and I danced
in the middle of the bathroom—
the entire final dance
from the tango class we took
at the gym in New Haven,
with the air as you.

I wasn't picturing you,
I didn't smell your damp hair—
don't imagine that I'm living
in memory.

Whatever I am, it is good at cutting meat.
The trick is: *That's blood.*
If you focus your fingers on feeling it,
you cannot mistake yourself for the animal,
who cannot feel; you never cut yourself
if you give your life to the blood you shed.

4

I know you've been waiting for disintegration,
but it just doesn't seem to be coming.

I need to go out to gather some berries.
No more meat: I've adopted your diet.

All this time, I thought my shedding
would expose a core,
I thought I would at least know myself,

but these mild passions, all surface, keep erupting now
like acne—or like those berries on a bush.

Don't ask me to name them—
I've never been that kind of guy.
Red berries—sour, sticky.
If you really want to know,
come here, just try them.

Red as earth,
red as a dying berry,
red as your lips,
red as the last thing I saw
and whatever next thing I will see.

Dear Sarah,

It meant so much to me to read with you, and to drink the soup you brought me yesterday. And to sit and laugh with you. You are one of the most special and rare sparkles of mind on earth right now, and I get to love you and be your friend. And that heals me and is a hothouse for the good that grows in me.

I hope I have a daughter. And that she's like you—wanting always to do good, always, and with no fear or panic motivating it, just with the dogged certainty that love is worth investing in. I hope she's funny like you. I hope she's funny like you, but not exploding like you.

Love,
Max

P.S. I mean that you are not exploding and I want her to be not exploding too. Grammar is funny.

Your essays in some strange way made me write a peripatetic lecture poem to my nephew.

A WALK WITH MY NEPHEW, WHO HAS ASKED
ABOUT BEING A GOOD MAN

Willpower is of course, breakable,
has been broken, in everyone, everything,

but it always comes back to the scratch at the screen door,
a dark red shape in its mouth,

brought back from abandon.

Perseverance, character: all death's other adversaries
are like this too, coming and going with the food, the noise—

in a storm they bolt out, or perhaps back in.
Look at what they're up against:

If death builds a sword ever more abrupt, flashing, invisible,
then what kind of shield do you expect us to build?

There's a black hallway we're all dipping into and out of,
all our souls slamming doors like in *Scooby-Doo*.

And he doesn't ever *get* us.
We just leave parts behind the doors

that we sometimes stumble back on again
if we happen to try the same door.

And eventually? Enough gets left behind.

Heaven? Sure there's still Heaven.
It's like this:

A fish leaps out of the water
and onto some grass by the roadside.

He can move so fast out there,
without water crushing his spine.

It's like discovering he's a guitar string,
meant to go faster than he'd realized—

all the gut he is sweetening
beyond reason into a note

as his body finds its place
in the silver flash that shuts out his mind,

out of air. Though there's more air now
than he even knows what to do with—

he melts in it like a waffle cone.
This isn't helping, I can tell.

Take this pill instead.
Somebody guessed just what life was like,

and then made a pill for it.
It's my favorite—vanilla I think.

Don't you worry, all that scared old sweat
will be washed away with fresh white new sweat.

Dearest Max,

You sounded wonderful on the phone yesterday. I went to hear Vivaldi's *Four Seasons* with Tony last night at the Philharmonic. I thought of you. I think it is one of the most beautiful pieces of music, and one of the most profound. You can hear the natural world in it, and our relationship to it. And I also think it's one of the most Taoist pieces of music I've ever heard. The seasons go on inhabiting the seasons, as fully as ever, and there is no end to it.

No end, I swear by all that is holy, only the silence in between the movements. You know those silences in which the educated audience members at concerts don't applaud? Because they know it is a "movement" that's just ended and not the end of a song? I think or hope that's what death is. The silence between movements; those who don't know any better applaud, but those who know music more intimately sit in silence and wait for the next movement to begin.

Brave Max, in pain Max, good Max.

Please give Victoria and Elizabeth and your mom a kiss for me.

I am coming to California in July and want to see you.

Love,
Sarah

And Max wrote back:

Lovely email. Love you. Talk tomorrow?

We did talk. We talked about our book. We talked about his book. He would write me short emails and say,

Sarahdear, I wish I had life of my own to report, but I've given you all the happy bits in texts. Give me some hope. And Anna. And William. Tell me what is happening with you and Tony.

Love,
Zesty Pepperjack Sauce

I would oblige him. When he said "give me some hope," he was joking—meaning, *give me some stories about your daughter Hope*, and *perhaps give me some hope*. I tried to distract him with domestic details, like:

Dear Zesty Jack,

Things over here are all about the end of kindergarten and fourth grade.

Debates about whether to bring kids to the annual water gun fight that celebrates the end of the school year, given the tragedy in Orlando.

Small domestic labors like putting new shelves in closets
and throwing out old baby blankets.

Theatrical labors like casting.

Reading Maggie Nelson: "the poetry of the future will
be nutritious and opulent. justifications for its existence
will no longer be interesting."

You might enjoy, if you did not catch it, that Lin-
Manuel Miranda brought the house down with a
SONNET at the Tony Awards, a sonnet, I tell you!

That July we also tried to wrap up more public ventures, like
an interview I did with Max to help celebrate the forthcoming publication of *Four Reincarnations*. I asked Max:

How can the poetry world reclaim the world of the
spirit in the secular age?

And Max answered:

Secularity has done a lot to challenge our relationship to
anything supernatural. But spirituality, at least to me, is
not supernatural, it's paranatural, or sometimes natural.

Spirituality doesn't require us to pray a number of times
a day, or accept any particular cosmological order, or
even to believe in things that there isn't proof for. All

spirituality asks is that we put ourselves in situations that feel holy. That take our breath away and make us go: I can't believe my luck to be part of something as beautiful as life.

✳

That month, interviews were copyedited. Blurbs were finalized. Max wrote an introduction to our book of letters that June and sent it to me. I offer it to you with some hesitation and embarrassment about Max's hyperbolic compliments; my impulse is to edit them out, but it was Max's introduction to our book, and I wanted to give you his own words:

> I saw my first Sarah Ruhl play when I was sixteen, as a treat after a bad round of chemotherapy. The play was Dead Man's Cell Phone. I'd never seen anything like it. It was a poem made of bodies and lights and tables and chairs. In the closest the show gets to a love scene, a man and woman express their love for paper, for stationery. It was loony, heartfelt, magnificent, pathetic—I felt so close to these people who confessed their hearts through objects. As their dialogue peaked, a fountain of paper erupted behind the desk they had crawled on top of. I wept. That night I called my girlfriend and told her yes, she was right, Sarah Ruhl was the best playwright ever, and I should've immediately read the plays she (my girlfriend) had bought

me when we'd started dating. When, six years later, I got a spot in Sarah's playwriting class I nearly crapped myself with excitement. In the seminar room she was all aikido, taking the momentum of a student's thought and amplifying it, and teaching us to amplify it, until the thought cart wheeled off into a notebook as a script nugget. Sarah wryly snuck problems under the rugs we weaved. If we had a passion, she gave us something to read. We mattered. On my super-passionate, super-amateurish scripts, Sarah'd leave gnomic notes. They somehow sent the writing in radical new directions, but they were completely nonjudgmental. I can't say I ever made much of a playwright, but God did my poetry get better. Then my cancer came back. And I thought I'd lose Sarah. She had a class to teach. A genius to be. But it was the opposite. We started writing. I was lonely, very lonely, and very scared. And Sarah is the holiest concatenation of Buddhist compassion and Catholic love that's ever warmed the cockles of my little atheist heart. She became my dharma guide, and my life project shifted. If I was to die, I would die full of love. Irreligious, but spiritually full. Over the next couple of years, we shared our histories. I met Sarah's children. She gave a blessing at my wedding and made my Eema a kugel so good it passed her Israeli muster. And we talked in person, on the phone, and through our letters, and became friends in the deep sense of You Are Not Alone. And we discussed True Love and

The Afterlife. And we never figured anything out. And that was what there was to figure out. And now, if I ever hug you, it is Sarah hugging you.

Then:

Everywhere. Time Unimportant.

Our letters became more fragmented as the summer days lengthened. I would send Max a poem, and Max, on morphine, would say, "Adored adored all thru my sleep and wake and loop." I had the good fortune of seeing Max many times over that summer. My work life brought me to Los Angeles that summer; I was grateful for the Fiji water bottle meetings at Hollywood studios, if only so that I could visit Max. Our long letters naturally turned into texts or phone calls or simply being in each other's presence, sometimes not talking, just sitting.

He revised his galleys and did press interviews from his blue steamer chair, his oxygen tank following him around. He had a poem published in the *New Yorker* that summer, "Poem to My Litter," and it was accompanied by an online video with a beautiful animation of Max reading the poem aloud. That was a victory.

Sometimes Max would text me about his upcoming book. On a bad day he would just text me: "Pain." Or: "Coughing up blood." On a good day he would get expansive, saying, "Do you think books want to talk to us? I walked outside for the first time today. It was so hot I felt like I was Moses in the desert. And I walked up a hill just like Moses." On a middling day, I'd say, "How are you?" And he'd say merely, "Upright."

✳

When I visited him, I would bring him the tastiest chocolate chip cookies I could find, because at the end, he had a singular taste for chocolate chip cookies. Sometimes I would hold his foot or a hand and he would sleep.

Sometimes Max would complain. Max was not a saint; he was an artist. In fact, one of my favorite Max traits was his penchant for revenge in matters of love and literature. When he detested another writer's work he would not pull punches, just as he would not hold back his ebullience when he loved a colleague's work. He had a series of revenge poems to an ex's new lover. He would say, "Revenge makes me feel very alive. 'Revenge is a dish best served cold' is bullshit." Sometimes he would rail about critics or bloggers who had misunderstood his work, and then comfort himself with the observation that *critic* rhymes with *dick*.

Sometimes Max would complain about the need of others to say goodbye to him at his own emotional expense. But he would always do so with good humor, as in: "Today my childhood nanny gripped me in her arms and said, 'You are breaking my heart, Max,' and then started to cross me hysterically. That was today's visit."

Sometimes we joked about death.

He texted me:

I mad some hand written cards
For b and mom
After I did
Did
Die

And I wrote, "Even autocorrect wants you to live."
"Ha," he said.

It became harder and harder for Max to talk; tumors were riddling his body, and his lungs filled with blood. He walked with great difficulty. One tumor was wrapped around his aorta. He had a terrible barking cough, and it was hard for him to catch his breath.

And yet his dear ones were so used to Max talking. He complained that the more he couldn't talk, the more questions people would ask him: "Like how does the wall work, how does paint dry, what is happening in this TV show?" I asked him, "And you want to be quiet?" He said,

> I do, but I also want to talk
> because it's how I love people
> And it's also how I live
> I love the sound of my own voice.

＊

He would ask me to visit him in a dream. Or he would tell me: "I'm meeting Mister Kevorkian. We'll figure out a nice hemlock."

＊

His texts became more fragmented, or more certain that his life would be a beautiful fragment. And he and I talked about how aesthetically, we both loved fragments. We would talk about the Japanese art of *wabi sabi*. Or Michelangelo's never-finished painting *The Manchester Madonna*; the impossible beauty of the unfinished figures in the background. And then he texted:

> Death doesn't seem soon
> It seems now
> like I'm actively scribbling out the last pages
> and while this is scary it also brings home how little I
> have to figure out
> God's an editor and he's gonna take this draft
> the book is written
> that's the part that actually means life happened.

✳

Three days of silence passed.

Max died that August, holding the hands of his wife and his mother. He was twenty-five.

The day before he died, he pulled his mother aside and said, "That's it. I can't write anymore."

He asked her, "Do you think I've fought hard enough?"

She assured him that he'd fought hard enough, always. Then she did the hardest thing a mother can do. She let him go.

And he let go.

I dreamed of Max a lot the fall after his death. Often I'd wake from a dream of Max and I'd be sitting up with a pencil in my hand, writing it down, urgently needing to remember his words. In one dream, he told me the moment of death was no worse than a colonoscopy. (I was having a colonoscopy that fall. It was just like Max to make a joke in a dream, and also to be concerned about my colonoscopy.)

I asked him if it was hard to be dead. He said: *Yes, it's hard to be dead. It's hard not to talk. But I am listening all the time.*

It comforts me to think of Max listening to us all the time.

All of us who miss Max have his writing forever, but we don't have his quicksilver, bold, loving, in-the-moment, joking, speaking presence. But might we still have his listening? And in having his listening, experience again, when we need it, his wide love?

Max once said in a conversation with his poet friend Justin Boening:

Death is the longest and most uncomfortable silence in existence. And it resolves in the most underwhelming utterance—even more silence. And the dying person imposes it on every single person they've ever known. Your loved ones think about dead you even when you're not around—they think about you for decades, for their whole lives if you loved them enough. Death gives you an audience for your uncomfortable silence that has no geographic or temporal constraint. It gives you a forever stage (at least until your audience goes extinct).

How to hold the grief of a teacher for a student? A friend for a friend? A writer for a writer?

I know many of Max's writer friends now feel a void when they are writing, without Max on the other end to read, to listen. Virginia Woolf once described poetry as "a voice answering a voice." For most poets, the voice answering the voice is an internal dialogue. Max had the gift of an internal voice, and also the gift of answering back to so many other poets.

Around this time I began to give more thought to ritual. I realized, startled, why people pray out loud—because it's easier for ghosts or God to hear you. That sometimes even ghosts need help knowing you're thinking of them. That's why you chant, mutter, light a candle, sing. Write.

I tried to write Max directly, like this:

Dear Max,

That forced smile you had the last time I saw you,
you never forced a smile before,
sitting up so straight, so tall—
showing me you could still smile, on top of your ravaged
body . . .

Dear Sarah,

I can no longer be reached at this body.
To email my new body,
please use my new address.

Dear Max,

But what is your new address?
I'm gonna miss you so bad,
I'm gonna miss you something awful . . .

Dear Sarah,

Sorry. You are being
bounced off my old address, my body.
Use my new address, dummy.

Dear Max,

Today I sat at our old spot at Atticus.
I ordered black bean soup and I made a little dish for you
and put it opposite me in case you're hungry.
I waited. I know you eat slow.

Dear Sarah,

I'm not hungry for soup. I'm hungry for a new address.
Stop using my old one.

Dear Max,

Okay, fine.
I will try a different address.

Your new address: Love?—unknown by postal service—
God Something Something, Air Something Lane or Terrace,
and me impersonating your voice—does it live here still?
Come back, come back, come back.

A year after Max died, I went to see Lama Pema, the same lama I ran into at Penn Station, so that he could do the traditional one-year chanting for Max. We called Max's mother so that she could hear the chanting. After Lama Pema chanted for Max, he said:

> It is very sad to die young, to die early. On the other hand, when you wake up from a dream, it doesn't matter how long the dream was. The important thing is that you wake up. You never remember how long the dream was.

Finally I had another dream of Max.

He told me: *Say hello to my mother.*

So I did.

Then, he told me: *Life is swaying, go back to life.*

And so I did.

Max still visits me in the strangest ways. I hesitate to tell you exactly how, because you'll think I am crazy—unless you, too, are visited by birds and paper hearts. I see profusions of paper hearts in the litter on the streets of New York City. And I assume they are from Max. At one particularly bleak moment, a perfectly sculpted tinfoil heart was put in my path. And I think: How could he make a tinfoil, or paper, or napkin heart from the ether? And then I think: Are there possibly this many heart-shaped pieces of garbage on the streets of New York? And finally I think: Is that partially Max's gift—to make me (and all of his fellow travelers) aware that even in things as unlikely as garbage and litter, still, there are hearts? In piles of garbage there is love. In bodies riddled with pain there is love. And poetry.

He said once to me in an interview:

> I can't think of anything right now I could immediately disqualify as the spiritual centerpiece of a poem.
> I don't think the spiritual world needs to be claimed or reclaimed by anyone or anything. Let religion lay hands upon it. Let secularity lay hands upon it. But let the hands be gently laid. Let anything that clasps offer the kind of prayer it wants to pray. Let this all be poetry.

Let this all be poetry.

Max had a wild gift of eloquence; he married this gift with his singular gift for listening. That Max could marry eloquence with listening made him wise.

When Max was twenty he wrote this, in his application to get into my playwriting class, about his desire to listen:

Give me some language and give me some listeners.
Let them do monstrous things that they don't intend
to do to make them happy and unhappy. We're all
just figuring out how to listen.

Afterword

Max didn't like cancer narratives. He didn't want to be known as the brave suffering poet who died too young. Max was always emotional, never sentimental. And that's why, when he was alive, we went back and forth about how to make our book of letters. I would argue for chronology; he would argue for selecting the best letters out of time, eliding the trivial details of an evolving friendship.

I felt that Max resisted chronology because he knew that the end of the narrative was not good. The end of this narrative meant he would die. By taking the letters out of order, in a Platonic sense, there was no beginning or middle and therefore no end. While Max was alive, we tried arranging the letters that way. But we both realized they didn't quite work aesthetically.

So I went back to that old saw—chronological order. I hope Max doesn't mind.

And, perhaps more interesting than either of us doing our literary speechifying, or spiritual sermonizing, is watching a friendship evolve through the trivia of time and place, and the vagaries of the body. Poetry is not embedded in such mundane concerns. It flies. Perhaps that's why ultimately I'm a playwright and not a poet—I traffic in mundane things like time and place. Max flies. He flies beyond any narrative of a boy who died too young. He wanted to be known for his work. For his words.

And so he should be, and so he will be.

Max's first book, *Four Reincarnations*, had a remarkable debut. He never felt the actual book in his hands, but he saw the cover, revised the galleys, and knew it was coming any day. In the book's first week in print, its sales had topped the *Odyssey* on Amazon's poetry section. That would have pleased Max. Many accolades were forthcoming—a rave from Helen Vendler among them—that placed Max's work in its proper context, along with other literary greats like Keats, Dickinson, Herbert. Max's mother still writes me to tell me of all his literary triumphs, saying with heavy irony, "More useless glory for Max," wishing she could hold him in her arms. Accolades are cold comfort.

Max and I always hoped that maybe this book would find its way into the hands of someone in need of comfort. I suppose comfort is a strange word for a book about a beautiful boy who becomes a young man, gets married, writes a book, and then dies way too young. But my hope is that Max's openness to life as he was dying, his passionate desire to write up until his very last moment, his ability to keep his sense of humor intact, his insistence on being concerned for everyone around him while he himself was in enormous pain, might offer solace. We are all going to die. Max did it sooner than he should have. But what is extraordinary is that he was a model for so many of how to live. And how to write. And how to hold living—and writing—in both hands. I think the best writers are concerned with writing and also with the question of how to live, and I think Max was the best kind of writer.

Now I hear Max over my shoulder, shouting, "Don't try

to draw a lesson from this. I know you're from the Midwest, but please, for the love of God, don't moralize! Don't elevate my illness over and above the rest of it. It's enough—my poetry and your grief—it's enough."

I agree. No lesson.

Max said in an interview once, "Humor isn't a shield, a repellant, it's almost a mnemonic device. It makes our sadness rhyme with joy."

Thank you for rhyming sadness with joy, Max.

And guess what? I'm on the quiet car right now. I'm still writing to you. I'll probably never stop.

Acknowledgments

Max's mother, Ari, was profoundly helpful in the process of making this book. Whether she was sending me pictures of Max, or allowing me and my family to stay in her house in Santa Barbara, and walk the same paths as Max walked, she was a beacon of grace and resilience. The loss she experienced is unfathomable, and I adore her indomitable spirit, and the way she tirelessly cares for Max's legacy. Elizabeth Metzger, beautiful poet and dear friend of Max, helped me figure out where different revisions of different Max poems were, and has been an extraordinary force of nature in preserving Max's poetry, and, just as importantly, sustained him through his last years. Thank you for all your guidance, Elizabeth. Amelia Roper, also Max's teacher, sent me early emails from Max, as well as providing encouragement for the project from the beginning. Other wonderful early readers of the letters: Bruce Ostler, who believed the early fragments could make a book; Beth Henley; Polly Noonan; Mark Tardi; and my mother, Kathleen Ruhl. The brilliant Daniel Slager and the whole team at Milkweed Editions (including the wonderful and compassionate editor Joey McGarvey) have been invaluable partners and champions of Max's work. Thank God they recognized the literary value of *Four Reincarnations* when they did, so that Max could revise his galleys and see that gorgeous cover before he died. Emma Feiwel and Mark Subias, both of whom had their own personal battles which they fought with bravery and grace last year—thank you for caring for this book. I'd like to thank Max's wife, Victoria, for giving him so much comfort and love in his last years. And I'd like to thank my remarkable husband, Tony, who understood my deep friendship with Max, and allowed it to flourish, and gave me comfort when Max died. Thank you to my children, who tolerated my having those long conversations on the phone with Max. And to Max's friends and my former students, Bonnie and Rachel, for being fellow travelers. And to Yale College and Marc Robinson, who asked me to teach my first undergraduate course, which allowed me to meet Max that fall. To my teachers—David Konstan and Paula Vogel—who helped me through when my father had cancer and I was far from home. And to the Sallie B. Goodman Retreat at the McCarter Theatre for allowing me space and time to write. And to Rebecca Taichman for allowing me to use her apartment to revise.

Max's acknowledgments tended to be pages long, and were he here to write this one, I'm sure it would have been longer—he loved you all so much, and you know who you are. His other teachers who lifted him up and supported him through his illness and are still helping to get Max's poetry into the world—Louise Glück, Dottie Lasky, Timothy Donnelly, Lucie Brock-Broido, geniuses all—and oh, Lucie. I didn't know you well, but Max did, and I can only hope the two of you are writing a long collaborative poem right at this moment. Thank you to the publications that allowed us to reprint Max's poems. And most of all, thank you, Max—your friendship is the treasure of a lifetime. Thank you for letting me finish our book.

Text and Illustration Credits

Thanks to *Narrative* for publishing "You know what a lee is" (as "Summer, Rhode Island"). Thanks also to the following publications, which published final versions of Max's poems in this book:

Horsethief: "Love Poem for Hera," "Your Next Date Alone"

Parnassus: "Earthquake Country before Final Chemotherapy," "Self-Portrait as Jesus," "The Final Voicemails"

Plume: "Giving Her 100%," "A Walk with My Nephew, Who Has Asked about Being a Good Man" (as "A Final Walk with My Nephew")

Other poems in this book were published in their final versions in Max's chapbook, *Aeons*, and his two complete collections, *The Final Voicemails* and *Four Reincarnations*:

Aeons: "Scan"

The Final Voicemails: "Listening, Speaking, and Breathing," "Your Next Date Alone," "Earthquake Country before Final Chemotherapy," "The Final Voicemails"

Four Reincarnations: "After *The Oldest Boy*" (as "Poem in Which My Shrink Is a Little Boy"), "Hospice" (as "Living It Up"), "Hi, Melissa"

Thanks to Jose Villa for permission to reproduce the photo on page 252, and to Polly Noonan for the photo on page 314.

You can find Victoria Ritvo's illustration of me and Max—and the exchange of letters that accompanies it—in *Berfrois*, at http://www.berfrois.com/2016/03/max-ritvo-sarah-ruhl/.

Zack DeZon

SARAH RUHL's plays include *In the Next Room, or the Vibrator Play* (Pulitzer Prize finalist, Tony Award nominee); *The Clean House* (Pulitzer Prize finalist, winner of the Susan Smith Blackburn Prize); *Passion Play, a cycle*; *Dead Man's Cell Phone* (winner of the Helen Hayes Award); *Stage Kiss*; *Dear Elizabeth*; *The Oldest Boy*; *How to Transcend a Happy Marriage*; *Eurydice*; and *For Peter Pan on Her 70th Birthday*. Her book of essays on the theater and motherhood, *100 Essays I Don't Have Time to Write*, was a *New York Times* Notable Book of the Year. She has been the recipient of a MacArthur Fellowship, the Helen Merrill Emerging Playwrights Award, the Whiting Writers' Award, the PEN/Laura Pels International Foundation for Theater Award for a midcareer playwright, and the Steinberg Award. She is currently on the faculty of the Yale School of Drama and lives in Brooklyn with her husband, Tony Charuvastra, and their three children.

Ashley Woo

MAX RITVO (1990–2016) was the author of two collections of poems, *Four Reincarnations* and *The Final Voicemails*, which were published by Milkweed Editions in 2016 and 2018. His chapbook, *Aeons*, was chosen by Jean Valentine to receive the Poetry Society of America Chapbook Fellowship in 2014. Ritvo's poetry has also appeared in the *New Yorker* and *Poetry*, among many other publications.

The Editor's Circle of Milkweed Editions

We gratefully acknowledge the following individuals for their annual leadership support of the literary arts.

Anonymous (1)
Mary Aamoth
Lynn Abrahamsen
Libby Andrus and
 Roby Thompson
Bill and Terry Ankeny
Brad and Marcia Ballinger
Keith and Mary
 Bednarowski
Barry Berg and
 Walter Tambor
Emilie and Henry
 Buchwald
Timothy and Tara Clark
Albert J. Colianni Jr. and
 Susan F. Colianni
Page and Jay Cowles
Cassie and Dan Cramer
Christopher and Katherine
 Crosby
Lisa Dalke and
 Kurt Bachmayer
Edward and Sherry Ann
 Dayton
Wendy Dayton
Veena Deo
Mary C. Dolan—The
 Longview Foundation
Beth and Kevin Dooley
Elizabeth Driscoll
Kirsten and Jack Driscoll
Peggy Driscoll and
 Rob Keeley
William Driscoll and
 Lisa Hoffman
Lisa Ferris and
 Kerry Marusich
Martha Gabbert
Charles and Barbara Geer
Daniel and Patricia Gerhan
Raeanna and Walter
 Gislason
Joanne and John Gordon
Geoff and Janny Gothro
Ellen Grace

John Gulla and
 Andrea Godbout
Richard Hall and
 Matt Nolan
Jayne and Al Hilde Jr.
Elizabeth and Edwin
 Hlavka
William and Cheryl Hogle
Harold and Peggy* Holden
 (in remembrance)
Jerry Irvin
Emily and George R. A.
 Johnson
Susan Kaufman and
 John Sullivan
Hart and Susan Kuller
Constance and Daniel
 Kunin
Chris Lawrence and
 Meghan McGrann
Donald and Elizabeth
 Leeper
Jim and Susan Lenfestey
Kathleen and Allen
 Lenzmeier
Adam and Maryann Lerner
Ross and Bridget Levin
Ann Litin and
 Claudio Hofstadter
Ann and Chris Malecek
Charles Marvin
Walter McCarthy and
 Clara Ueland
Robert and Vivian
 McDonald
Jorie and Keith Miller
Lucy and Bob Mitchell—
 The Longview
 Foundation
Ann and Alfred Moore
Kate Moos and
 Valerie Arganbright
Betsy Moran and
 Brian Johnson
Sheila C. Morgan

Chris and Jack Morrison
Helen Morrison
Kelly Morrison and
 John Willoughby
Matt Murphy and
 Maura Rockcastle
Carolyn and Bob Nelson
Robin B. Nelson
Wendy Nelson
Greg Page
Christopher Pearson and
 Amy Larson
Elizabeth Petrangelo and
 Michael Lundeby
Jörg and Angela Pierach
Patricia Ploetz
Janet Polli and Matt Ides
Margaret and Dan Preska
Pete Rainey
Melissa Raphan and Tom
 Rock Charitable Fund
Norman Rickeman and
 Kathy Murphy
Sandra Roe
Cheryl Ryland
Linda and Jesse Singh
Daniel Slager and
 Alyssa Polack
Stephen and Cynthia
 Snyder
Stephanie Sommer and
 Stephen Spencer
Sarah Stoesz and
 David Foster
Tracey Thayer Breazeale
 and Jeff Breazeale
Ruth Travis
Joanne Von Blon
Margot Walk
Cindy and Mark Welton
Eleanor and Fred Winston
Margaret and Angus*
 Wurtele (in
 remembrance)

milkweed
editions

Founded as a nonprofit organization in 1980,
Milkweed Editions is an independent publisher.
Our mission is to identify, nurture and publish
transformative literature, and build
an engaged community around it.

We are aided in this mission by generous individuals who make a gift to underwrite books on our list.
Special underwriting for *Letters from Max* was
provided anonymously.

milkweed.org

Interior design by Mary Austin Speaker
Typeset in Fournier

Fournier is a typeface created by the Monotype Corporation
in 1924, based on types cut in the mid-eighteenth century
by Pierre-Simon Fournier, a French typographer.
The specific cuts used as a reference for Fournier
are referred to as "St Augustin Ordinaire" in
Fournier's influential *Manuel Typographique*,
published in 1764 in Paris.